This Book belongs to

DRAW PAINT PRINT like the GREAT ARTISTS

Marion Denchars

LAURENCE KING

PUBLISHED IN 2014 by

LAURENCE KING PUBLISHING Ltd
361 - 373 CITY ROAD
LONDON EC1V 1LR
Tel + 44 20 7841 6900
Fax + 44 20 7841 6910
www.laurenceking.com
enquiries@laurenceking.com

A CATALOG RECORD OF THIS BOOK IS AVAILABLE FROM THE BRITISH LIBRARY.

ISBN 978-1-78067-2-816

Printed in China

In this book I have chosen some of my favorite artists who have been an important influence on me, helping me to develop my own style over the years. By exploring their techniques, I began to understand the essence of their work and how they see the world around them.

Every artist learns by looking at the work created by others, and then picks up bits of that and makes their own art in their own way. Through the artists in this book, you will discover new working methods and new ways of exploring image making.

It may be something as simple as using scissors rather than a pencil, or being fascinated by a new shape or a playful exercise to take your imagination somewhere unfamiliar.

I hope you enjoy learning from these artists as much as I have, both over the years and in the making of this book.

Marion Deuchars

"Creativity takes courage"

Henri Matisse

ART MATERIALS

A LIST OF BASIC ART MATERIALS

WHITE GLUE (OR GLUE STICK)

SCISSORS

CONSTRUCTION PAPER (in different sizes and colors)

RULER

PENCILS

COLORED PENCILS

PENS

TAPE

PAINTBRUSHES (different sizes)

CRAYONS OR PASTELS

PAINTS

DRAWING COMPASS

ERASER

PENCIL SHARPENER

WATER CONTAINER

PALETTE

INK

PENCILS

PENCILS COME IN ALL SHAPES AND SIZES. TRY TO HAVE A DIFFERENT RANGE, FROM HARD TO SOFT.

WATER SOLUBLE

This means when you add water they change from pencil to watercolor.

GRAPHITE PENCIL OR STICK

VERY GOOD FOR COVERING LARGE AREAS ON THE PAPER.

FELT-TIP PENS

COME IN ALL DIFFERENT SHAPES AND SIZES. TRY TO GET SOME THICK AND THIN ONES.

BRUSH PENS ARE USEFUL TOO

ERASERS

REGULAR ERASER (HARD)

PUTTY ERASER (SOFT)

Can be squeezed into shapes

DRAWING COMPASS

CHARCOAL IS SOFT, BLACK, AND VELVET LIKE TO DRAW WITH.

PAPER

CHALKS AND PASTELS

COME IN BEAUTIFUL COLORS. THEY HAVE A "PAINTING-EFFECT" WHEN YOU MIX OR BLEND THEM.

CONSTRUCTION paper / PHOTOCOPY paper / CARTRIDGE paper

(comes in different weights/thickness e.g.)

80 gms - light (ok for DRAWING)
300 gms - heavy (ok for PAINTING)

PALETTES

GOOD FOR MIXING
AND STORING PAINT

PLASTIC PALETTES

PAPER PALETTES ARE VERY USEFUL.
THEY ARE DISPOSABLE AND YOU
CAN KEEP PAINT WET FOR A FEW
DAYS BY PUTTING A PAPER
TOWEL ON TOP.

PAINTS

GOUACHE

An opaque watercolor paint. You cannot see the white of the paper through it.

ACRYLIC

A plastic-based paint. Mix with water to use it thick or thin. Very versatile.

POSTER/CRAFT

Ideal for posters, crafts, and school projects. It is a water-based paint and the least expensive to buy.

PAN OR TUBE

WATERCOLOR

A transparent paint, you can see the white of the paper through it.

ROUND

FLAT

POINTED

BRUSHES

HOG/BRISTLE – hard brushes, good for acrylic and poster paints
SYNTHETIC – cheaper but good all-rounders (all paints)
SABLE – soft. Expensive but high quality. (all paints)

MASKING TAPE

INK IS GREAT FOR DRAWING. IT COMES IN ALL DIFFERENT COLORS.

DIP PEN

USE A "DIP PEN," BRUSH, STICK, OR CARD!

A good pair of SHARP SCISSORS. You can also buy safety scissors.

VERY USEFUL FOR TAPING PAPER TO DESK. ALSO FOR HIDING OR "MASKING" AREAS ON THE PAPER.

OLD JARS ARE GOOD AS WATER CONTAINERS

GLUE

GLUE STICK, OR PVA (WHITE GLUE)

ROLLERS

GREAT FOR PAINTING LARGE AREAS. OR USE ONE TO MAKE YOUR OWN COLORED PAPER.

Joan Miró

YOU CAN RECOGNIZE MUCH OF JOAN MIRÓ'S WORK AS IT LOOKS VERY CHILDLIKE, WITH BRIGHT COLORS AND THICK BLACK OUTLINES. HE LIKED TO USE MANY DIFFERENT TEXTURES AND MATERIALS IN HIS WORK TO CREATE DIFFERENT "FEELINGS." I'VE COMBINED A TEXTURED, PAINTED BACKGROUND WITH A BLACK CRAYON LINE, A SMUDGE CIRCLE, AND A PAINTED SOLID CIRCLE TO SHOW HOW ALL THESE MARKS, ALTHOUGH NOT RELATED, CAN WORK TOGETHER IN ONE PAINTING.

AUTOMATIC DRAWING

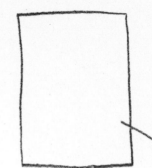

WHITE PAPER

MIRÓ PRACTICED "AUTOMATIC DRAWING," WHERE THE HAND IS ALLOWED TO MOVE "RANDOMLY" ACROSS THE PAPER, TO MAKE MANY OF HIS PAINTINGS.

WHAT YOU NEED

WHITE PAPER
THICK BLACK CRAYON
COLORED PENS, PENCILS,
OR PAINT

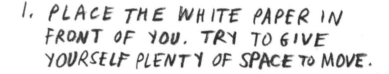

1. PLACE THE WHITE PAPER IN FRONT OF YOU. TRY TO GIVE YOURSELF PLENTY OF SPACE TO MOVE.

2. CLOSE YOUR EYES.

3. USING THE BLACK CRAYON DRAW QUICKLY ACROSS YOUR PAPER USING A COMBINATION OF STRAIGHT LINES AND SQUIGGLY ONES.

   * YOU CAN LOOK TO MAKE SURE YOU ARE DRAWING ON THE PAPER and NOT YOUR DESK!

4. COLOR IN THE RANDOM SHAPES YOU HAVE MADE IN BRIGHT COLORS.

COLOR IN THESE SHAPES:

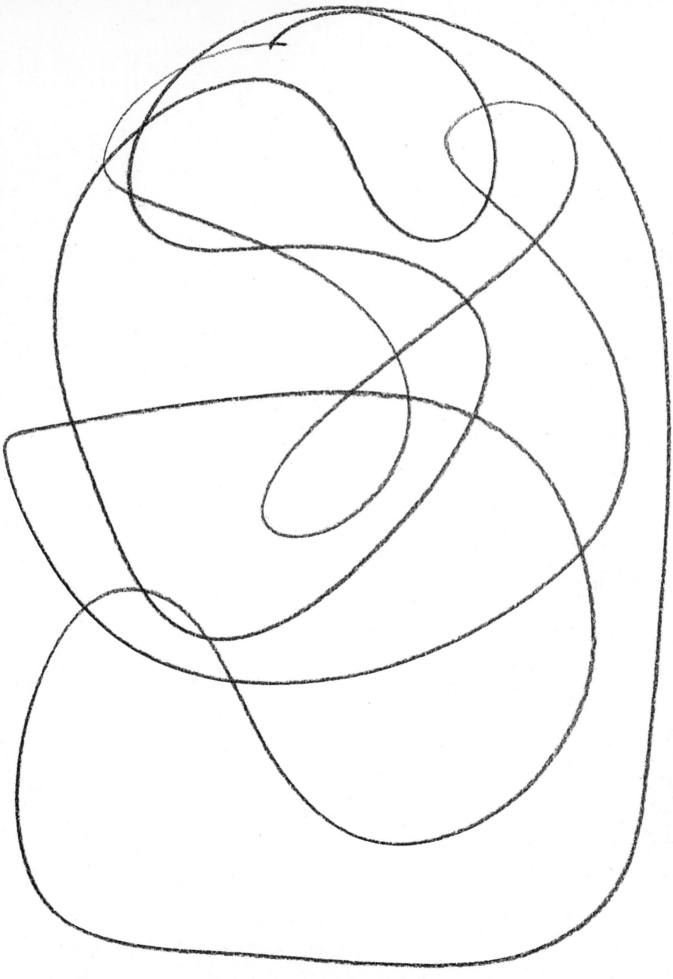

PRACTICE AUTOMATIC DRAWING.
  COLOR IN THE SHAPES.

CLOSE YOUR EYES!
↓

EXPERIMENTS AND MARK-MAKING

WHEN I LOOK AT SOME OF MIRÓ'S PAINTINGS, WHAT FASCINATES ME ARE THE DIFFERENT PAINT TECHNIQUES WITHIN ONE IMAGE. THEY LOOK LIKE HE WAS PLAYING WITH AND ENJOYING THE MATERIALS.

TRY TO MAKE YOUR OWN EXPERIMENTS WITH MATERIALS AND MARK-MAKING IN THE BOXES.

"WATERY" PAINT
WATERCOLOR OR "WATERED-DOWN" POSTER OR ACRYLIC PAINT

"WATERY" PAINT

SOLID PAINT

SOLID PAINT

* SOLID, THICK POSTER OR ACRYLIC PAINT. YOU MIGHT NEED A FEW LAYERS. YOU SHOULD NOT "SEE THROUGH" IT.

PAINTED DRY LINE

PAINTED DRY LINE

PAINTED WET LINE

PAINTED WET LINE

CRAYON OR SOFT PENCIL

CRAYON OR SOFT PENCIL

SOLID HARD EDGE

SOLID HARD EDGE

WATERY, TRANSPARENT

WATERY, TRANSPARENT

PENCIL LINES

PRESSING DOWN SOFTLY

PRESSING DOWN HARD

PRESSING DOWN SOFTLY

PRESSING DOWN HARD

FAST LINE

SLOW LINE

FAST LINE

SLOW LINE

FAST LINE

SLOW LINE

FAST LINE

SLOW LINE

COPY THE MARK-MAKING IN THE BOXES.

ROUGH LINE

SMOOTH LINE

ROUGH LINE

SMOOTH LINE

ANGRY LINE

HAPPY LINE

ANGRY LINE

HAPPY LINE

ONCE YOU HAVE EXPERIMENTED IN MARK-MAKING, TRY TO "COMBINE" THEM: SOFT CRAYON ON TOP OF (DRIED!) WATERY PAINT; THICK PAINT SHAPES ON TOP OF WATERY PAINT; FAST LINES NEXT TO SLOW LINES.

TEXTURES

MIRÓ LIKED TO USE BRIGHT, SIMPLE COLORS IN HIS WORK: RED, YELLOW, BLUE, GREEN, AND BLACK. HIS WORK LOOKS PLAYFUL AND CHILDLIKE AND WAS INFLUENCED BY SURREALISM. HE COMBINED ABSTRACT OR MADE-UP SHAPES WITH RECOGNIZABLE OBJECTS—A MOON, A LADDER, A STAR, A WOMAN. I LIKE THE DIFFERENT TEXTURES HE USES IN HIS WORK. TRY TO COPY SOME OF THESE TEXTURES.

WHAT YOU NEED

COLOR FELT-TIP PENS OR MARKERS
CRAYON, CHALKS OR CHARCOAL
CHINAGRAPH PENCIL (WAX PENCIL)
WHITE PAPER
COLORED PAPER
PENCIL

YOU CAN BUILD UP TONE IN MANY WAYS. HERE ARE SOME OF THEM:
TEXTURE WITH PENS, OR MARKERS.

ONE DIRECTION   CROSS HATCH

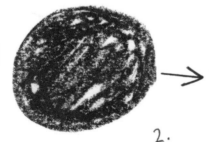

1.   2.

SIDE OF PENCIL

SOLID TONE

1. USE A CRAYON, CHARCOAL, CHINAGRAPH PENCIL, OR PAINT TO MAKE YOUR SHAPE.

2. FILL IN THE SHAPE, GOING OVER THE SHAPE SEVERAL TIMES UNTIL SOLID.

COLOR IN USING DIFFERENT TEXTURES

TEXTURES

SMUDGE MARKS

1. USE A CRAYON, CHALK, OR CHARCOAL TO DRAW YOUR SHAPE.

2. FILL IN THE SHAPE, GOING OVER THE SHAPE SEVERAL TIMES TO BUILD UP A NICE THICK LAYER OF COLOR.

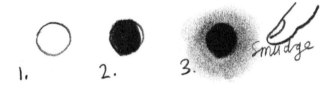

1.   2.   3.   *smudge*

3. NOW RUB FINGER OVER IT TO CREATE SOFT EDGES.

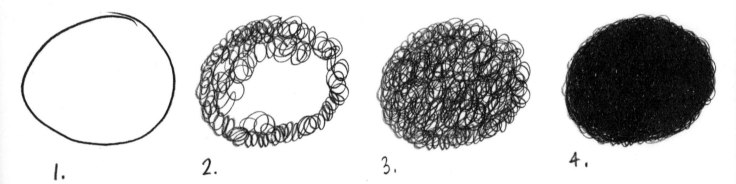

1.   2.   3.   4.

1. LIGHTLY DRAW A CIRCLE SHAPE WITH CRAYON OR PENCIL.

2. START FILLING THE CIRCLE SHAPE WITH CIRCULAR SCRIBBLES.

3. KEEP SCRIBBLING UNTIL FULL.

4. NOW KEEP SCRIBBLING ON TOP OF SCRIBBLES UNTIL YOU HAVE A FILLED-IN DARK BLACK CIRCLE.

YOU NOW HAVE A BLACK CIRCLE WITH TEXTURE. IT IS NOT FLAT OR OPAQUE BUT HAS A "MOVING" QUALITY TO IT.

COLOR IN USING DIFFERENT TEXTURES. COMPLETE THE IMAGE USING SOFT OR HARD LINES, ANGRY LINES, OR HAPPY LINES.   →

Philip Guston

PHILIP GUSTON WAS A SELF-TAUGHT ARTIST WHO HAD PHASES OF DOING
FIGURATIVE PAINTING (WITH RECOGNIZABLE IMAGES) AND ABSTRACT PAINTING
(WITHOUT RECOGNIZABLE IMAGES). FINALLY HE DECIDED TO DRAW WHAT HE
LIKED, AND THIS WORK HAD A CARTOONY STYLE IN A LANGUAGE OF
HIS OWN. INSPIRED BY GUSTON, I'VE MADE A CARTOON-STYLE
PAINTING WHERE I'VE DRAWN WHATEVER I LIKED.

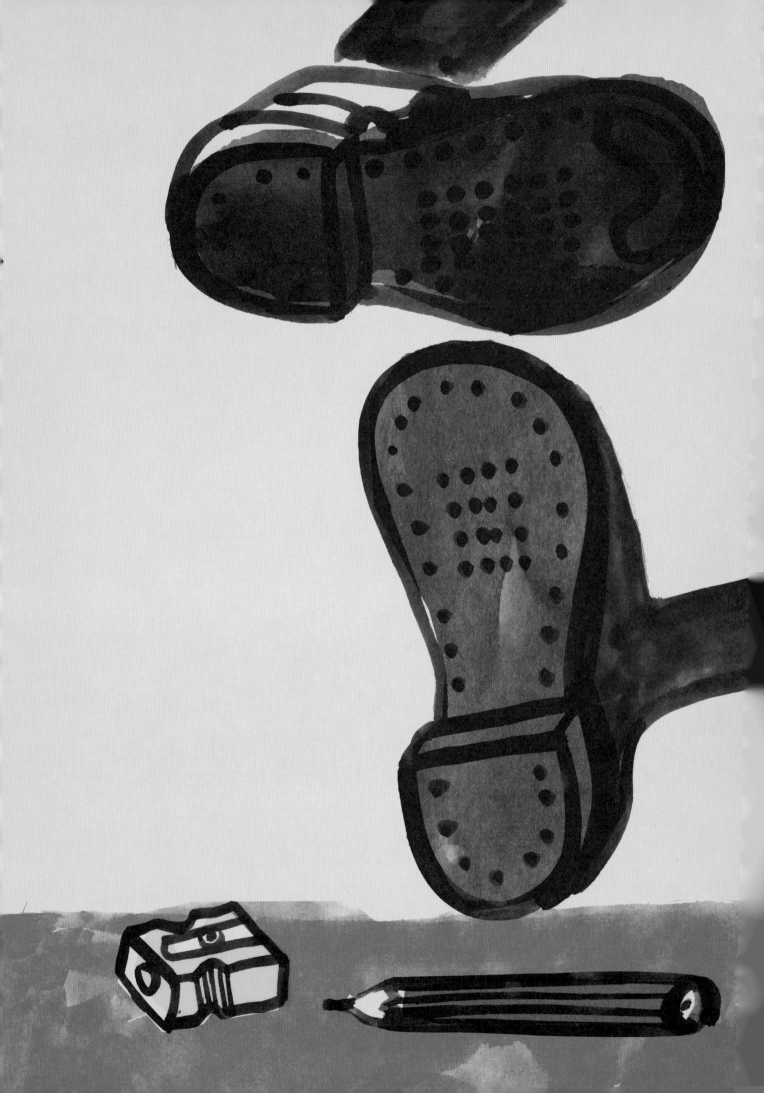

DRAW WHAT YOU LIKE

GUSTON'S WORK LOOKED CARTOONY, BUT HE DREW THINGS THAT WERE IMPORTANT TO HIM. HE DREW WHATEVER HE LIKED AND DID NOT CARE IF OTHERS DISLIKED IT.

DRAW AN OBJECT THAT HAS SENTIMENTAL VALUE TO YOU. HERE IS MY TOY DINOSAUR, BUT IT CAN BE ANYTHING. DRAW IT AT DIFFERENT SIZES AND ANGLES, GET TO KNOW EVERY DETAIL. IT IS ONLY BY LOOKING VERY HARD AT SOMETHING THAT WE TRULY SEE IT.

DESTROYED DRAWINGS

PHILIP GUSTON said:

"Destruction of paintings is crucial to me."

Here is a drawing I've painted over.

When we make a drawing or painting and we feel it goes wrong, we have a choice. We can rip it up and destroy it, or we can paint over it.

Painting over something to "destroy" it can be a very good starting point for a new drawing or painting. It can help take away the fear of a "blank sheet of paper."

Now you draw on top of my drawing.

Try it the next time you make a picture you are unhappy with.
Drawings with a "history" behind them can be more interesting.

Here is a drawing I've painted over. Draw on top of it with white.

Draw something and paint over it.   ↓

Jivya Soma Mashe

JIVYA SOMA MASHE IS AN ARTIST AND MEMBER OF THE WARLI TRIBE OF
INDIA. HIS MOTHER DIED WHEN HE WAS SEVEN AND FOR SEVERAL YEARS HE
WOULD COMMUNICATE ONLY BY DRAWING IMAGES IN THE DUST. IN HIS ART
HE USES CIRCLES, SQUARES, AND TRIANGLES TO ILLUSTRATE THE WORLD
AROUND HIM. HERE I'VE COPIED HOW MASHE MADE A HUMAN BODY BY JOINING
TWO TRIANGLES AT THE TIP THEN MAKING A CIRCLE PATTERN WITH THEM TO
REPRESENT THEIR WORLD.

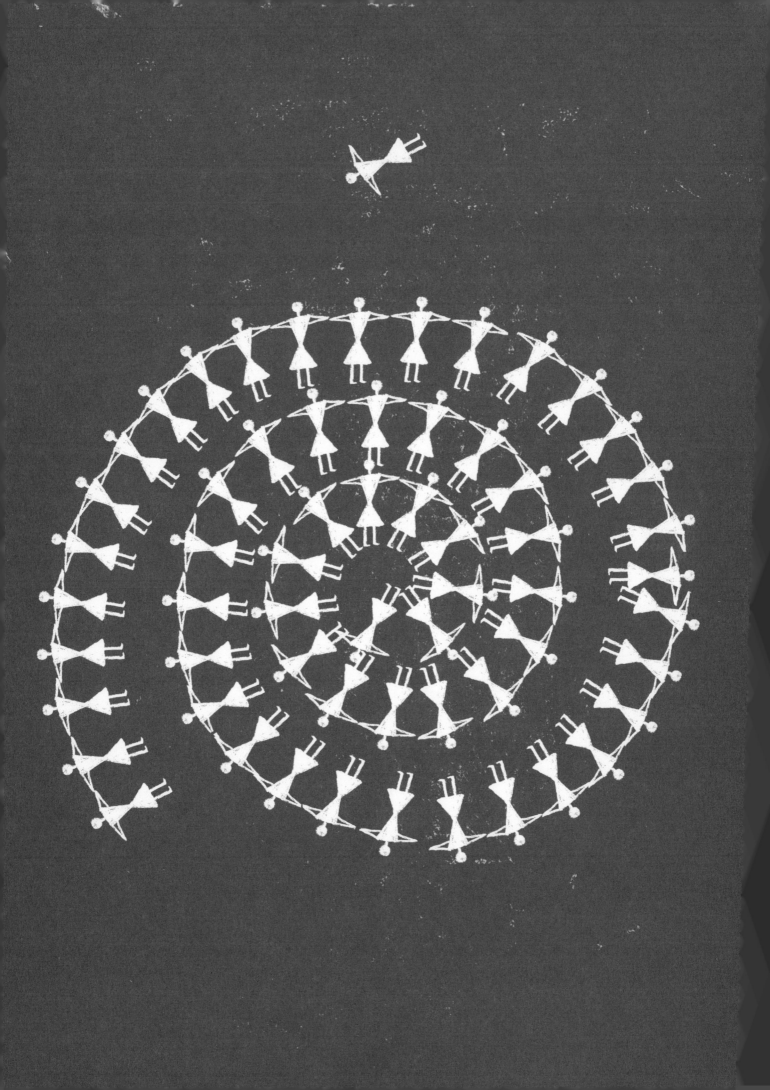

WARLI TRIBAL ART

THE WARLI TRIBE FROM INDIA USES VERY SIMPLE FORMS TO MAKE THEIR ART, WHICH DEPICTS HUNTING, DANCING, SOWING, AND HARVESTING, AND IS NORMALLY PAINTED ON THEIR MUD WALLS.

THE WARLI ONLY USE WHITE FOR THEIR PAINTINGS, MADE FROM RICE PASTE GUM AND WATER. A PIECE OF BAMBOO IS CHEWED AT THE END TO FORM A BRUSH.

THE WARLI USE

CIRCLES, SQUARES, TRIANGLES

INSPIRED BY THE MOON AND SUN

MEANING SACRED ENCLOSURE

BASED ON THE MOUNTAINS AND TREES

COPY THE WAY THE WARLI DRAW PEOPLE (MADE WITH 2 TRIANGLES) AND SEE IF YOU CAN JOIN THEM TOGETHER ON THIS SPIRAL SHAPE. USE WHITE PAINT OR A WHITE GEL PEN. →

TWO TRIANGLES, JOINED AT THE TIP.   ADD HEAD, ARMS, LEGS.

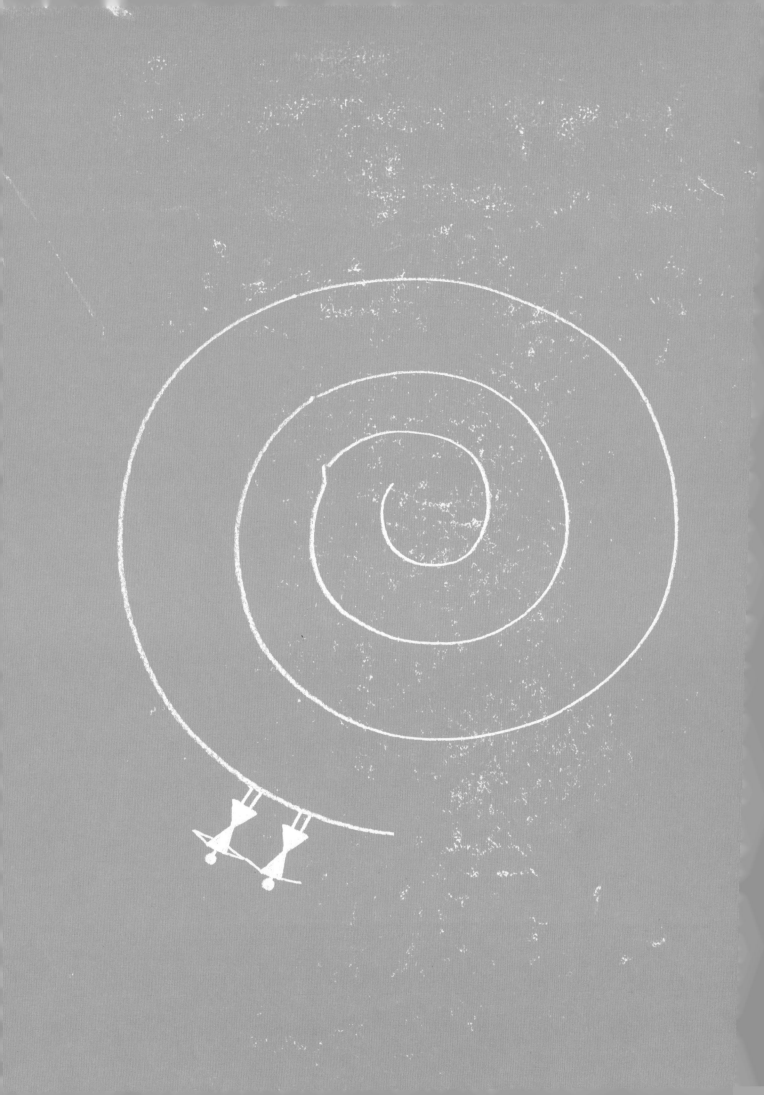

MAKE YOUR OWN ART USING VERY SIMPLE
REPETITIVE SHAPES AROUND THE TRIANGLE
AND SQUARE.

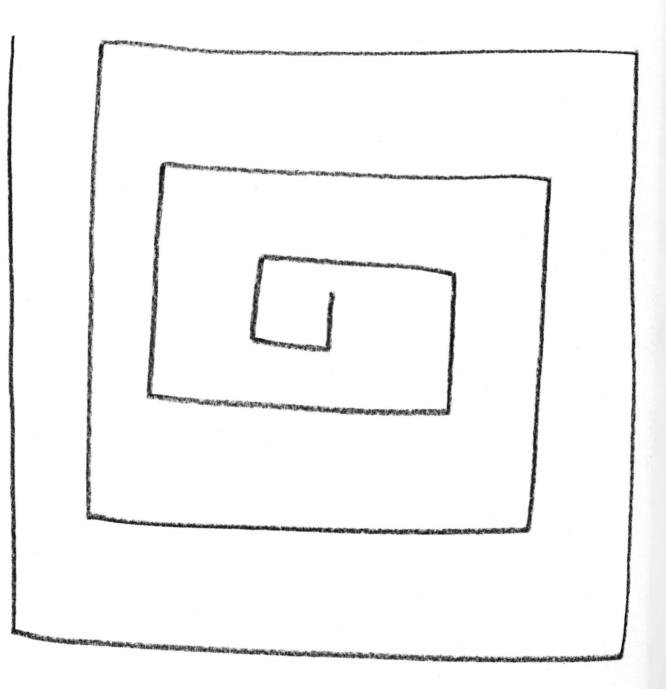

CUT OUT SOME CIRCLES, SQUARES,

USE COLORED PAPER IN ALL DIFFERENT SIZES.
ARRANGE THEM TO MAKE DIFFERENT
PATTERNS. USE THE PAPER ON THE NEXT PAGE.

USE A STENCIL
TO CUT OUT SOME
NEAT CIRCLES.

YOU CAN CUT A CIRCLE IN HALF
TO MAKE A HALF-CIRCLE AND
GIVE YOU MORE PATTERN
POSSIBILITIES.

and TRIANGLES

HOW MANY CHARACTERS OR PATTERNS CAN YOU MAKE USING CUT OUT
CIRCLES, TRIANGLES, AND SQUARES AS THE MAIN ELEMENTS

WHAT YOU NEED

COLORED PAPER
PENCILS
SCISSORS
GLUE

GLUE THEM HERE:

MAKE PATTERNS BY COLORING IN.

MAKE PATTERNS BY COLORING IN

MAKE PATTERNS BY COLORING IN

THE WARLI USE SIMPLE ANIMAL FORMS AND SYMBOLS.

MAKE YOUR OWN PEOPLE, ANIMALS, AND SYMBOLS,
USING TRIANGLES TO START.   ↓

MAKE YOUR OWN SIMPLE PATTERNS INSIDE THE SQUARE.
USE WHITE PAINT OR A GEL PEN.

PEOPLE AND ANIMALS
MADE FROM 2 TRIANGLES

CAN YOU DRAW WHERE THEY ARE?
IN A PARK, A STREET, A MARKET?

HOW MANY CHARACTERS CAN YOU MAKE?

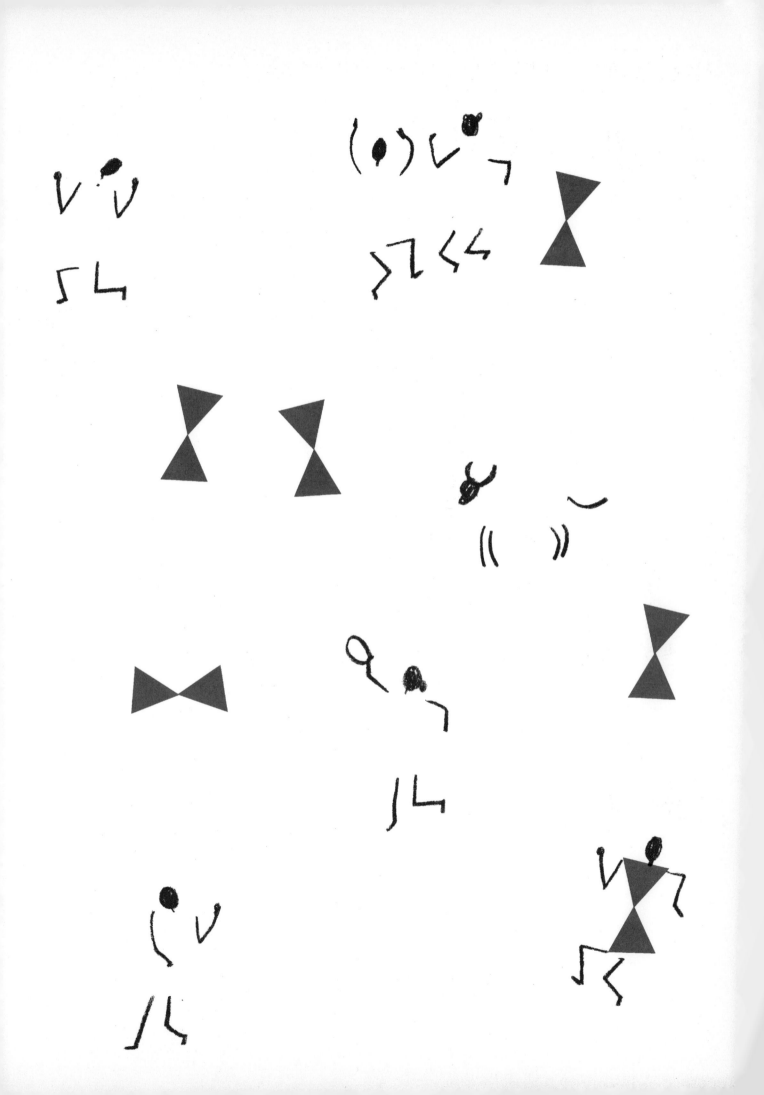

Eduardo Chillida

EDUARDO CHILLIDA WAS A SCULPTOR AND A MASTER OF USING BOTH POSITIVE AND NEGATIVE SPACE. WHEN I LOOK AT HIS WORK MY EYE IS DRAWN TO THE NEGATIVE (EMPTY) SPACES. HERE I'VE CREATED SHAPES ON THE PAGE IN THE STYLE OF CHILLIDA. WHICH IS THE STRONGER SHAPE TO YOU? THE WHITE SPACE OR THE BLACK SPACE? LET YOUR EYE PLAY BETWEEN THE TWO.

COLOR IN THE GRAY SHAPES WITH BLACK CRAYON OR PENCIL.

NOW KEEP THE SHAPES WHITE AND
COLOR THE BACKGROUND BLACK.

POSITIVE SPACE
NEGATIVE SPACE

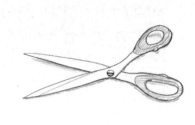

WHAT YOU NEED

BLACK PAPER (small)
WHITE PAPER (large)
SCISSORS
A RULER (IF YOU WANT)
GLUE

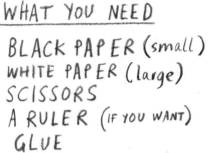

DRAW A PENCIL GRID ON YOUR WHITE PAPER. CUT UP YOUR BLACK PAPER INTO SHAPES A BIT LIKE THESE. THEY LOOK A LITTLE LIKE A JIGSAW PUZZLE.

NOW REARRANGE THESE ON THE LARGER SHEET OF WHITE PAPER. THERE IS NO RIGHT WAY OR WRONG WAY, BUT WHEN YOU ARE ARRANGING AND PLAYING WITH THE BLACK SHAPES, TRY TO CONCENTRATE ON THE WHITE SPACES IN BETWEEN. THESE SPACES ARE JUST AS IMPORTANT.

WHEN YOU ARE HAPPY WITH THE ORDER OF YOUR SHAPES. STICK THEM DOWN. NOW YOU WILL HAVE A PICTURE WHERE YOU WON'T BE ABLE TO TELL IF IT'S A PIECE OF WHITE PAPER WITH BLACK SHAPES OR VICE VERSA.

CHILLIDA USED THIS TECHNIQUE VERY OFTEN
AS A STEP TOWARD MAKING 3-D SCULPTURES.

CUT OUT BLACK PAPER SHAPES OF YOUR OWN
AND STICK THEM DOWN HERE. KEEP THINKING
ABOUT THE POSITIVE AND NEGATIVE SPACES.

Sonia Delaunay

WHEN I THINK OF SONIA DELAUNAY, I SEE BRILLIANT COLORS, AND
CIRCLES, CIRCLES, AND MORE CIRCLES. SHE PAINTED THEM, DREW
THEM, CUT THEM OUT, AND CHOPPED THEM UP. SHE PUT THEM
ON EVERYTHING FROM PAINTINGS TO THEATER COSTUMES. IN THIS
PICTURE I'VE CUT OUT A RED CIRCLE AND A BLACK CIRCLE FROM
COLORED PAPER, CUT THEM DOWN THE MIDDLE, AND USED TWO
HALVES TO MAKE A DELAUNAY-STYLE CIRCLE COMPOSITION.

CIRCLES, CIRCLES, CIRCLES

WHAT YOU NEED

Old lids
Paint
Paper palette or old trays

1. Collect old lids from bottles, cups, old jars. paper towel, tops of pens. Anything circular.

2. Mix bright-colored paint on a palette or tray (or old magazine paper).

3. Dip a circular object into the paint and "print" it by pressing down onto your paper.

4. Keep repeating with different sizes and colors until you have filled the page with circles.

COMPLETE THE CIRCLES BY ADDING MORE COLOR CIRCLES.

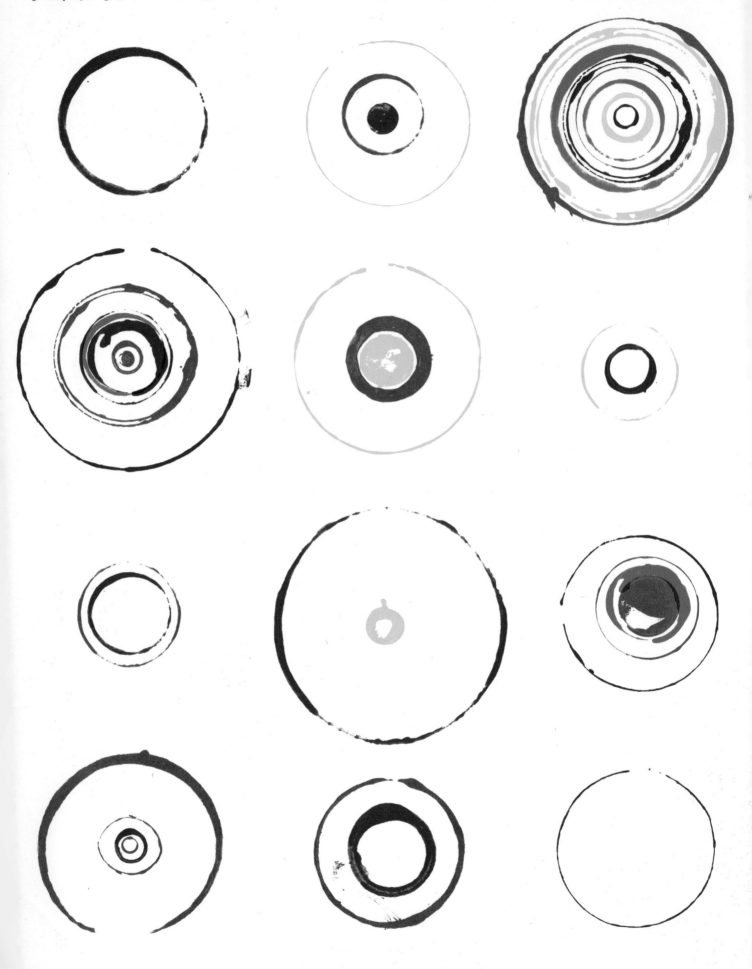

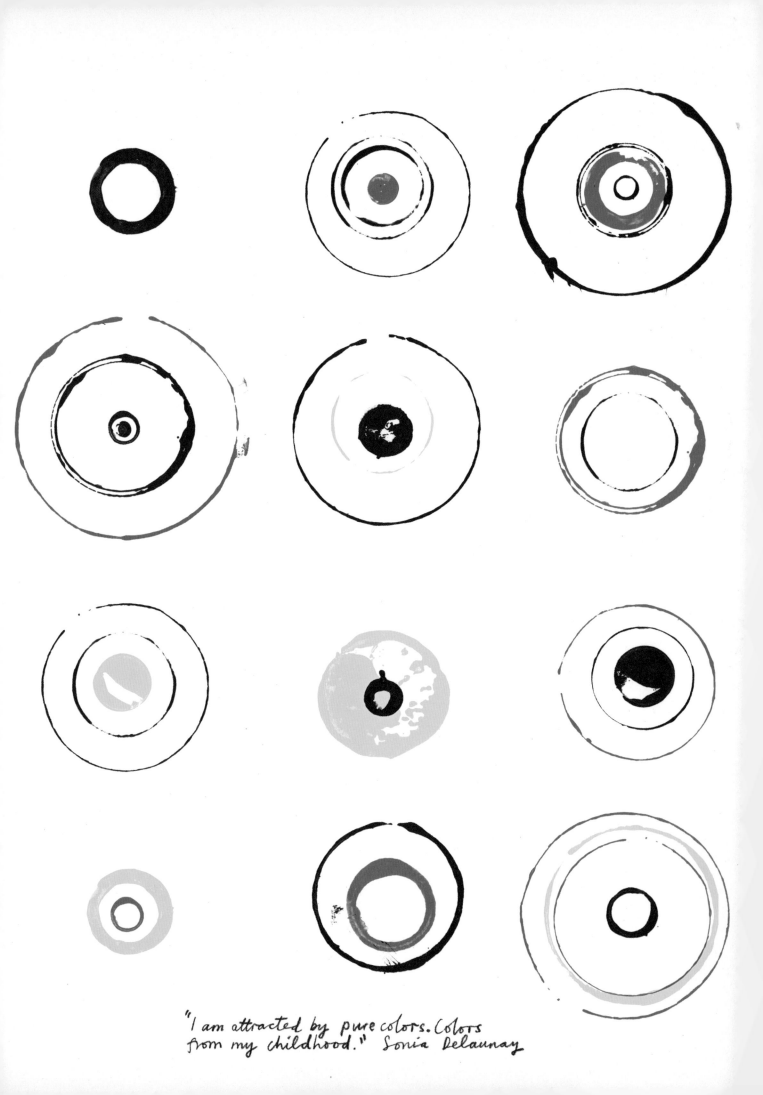

"I am attracted by pure colors. Colors from my childhood." Sonia Delaunay

MAKE MORE CIRCLES!

COLOR IN THE CIRCLES
THAT HAVE BEEN SPLIT
UP WITH LINES.

Cut Paper Circles

WHAT YOU NEED

COLORED PAPER (IN STRONG COLORS)

SCISSORS

COMPASS (OR CIRCLE TEMPLATES LIKE LIDS)

GLUE

1. CUT OUT DIFFERENT-SIZED CIRCLES FROM COLORED PAPER.

2. CUT SOME OF THEM IN HALF.

3. NOW TRY TO MAKE NEW CIRCLES, JOINING DIFFERENT COLORS AND SIZES TOGETHER.

4. GLUE THEM ONTO COLORED PAPER ON THE NEXT PAGE.

HALF-CIRCLE FLIPPED OVER

CIRCLES
ON TOP OF ONE
ANOTHER

JOIN THEM AT AN
ANGLE.

SONIA DELAUNAY MADE DESIGNS FOR FASHION
AND THEATER. CUT UP YOUR PRINTED CIRCLES
TO MAKE YOUR OWN COSTUME DESIGNS.

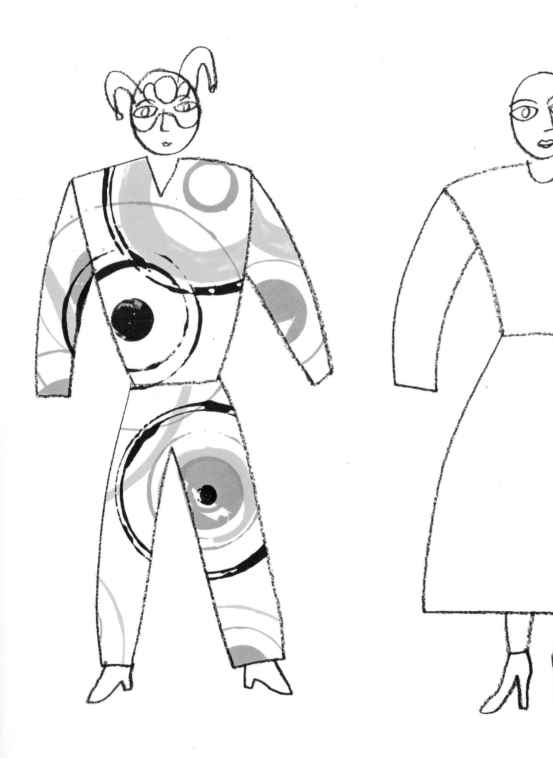

Salvador Dalí

SALVADOR DALÍ WAS A PAINTER WHO WAS KNOWN FOR HIS ODD
BEHAVIOR AND BENDY MUSTACHE AS MUCH AS FOR HIS WORK.
HE HAD A CRAZY SENSE OF HUMOR AND PLAYED GAMES AND
PRACTICAL JOKES IN HIS ART. DALÍ CREATED ARTWORKS WHERE
UNEXPECTED THINGS HAPPEN WITH THINGS YOU DON'T EXPECT TO
SEE TOGETHER. IN THIS DALÍ-INSPIRED ARTWORK, I'VE PAINTED
AN EYE ON CRUTCHES IN A LANDSCAPE SURROUNDED BY ANTS.

ART GAMES

DALI BELONGED TO AN ART GROUP CALLED THE "SURREALISTS," meaning SUPER REAL. THEY PLAYED MANY GAMES IN THEIR WORK. SOME WERE CHILDREN'S GAMES THAT THEY REINVENTED, WITH EXOTIC OR ODD-SOUNDING NAMES, AND USED AS DEVICES TO CREATE ART.

HERE ARE SOME.

CALLIGRAMME

shrink

bumpy

WORDS OR LETTERS MAKE UP
A SHAPE CONNECTED TO THE
SUBJECT.

HERE I'VE USED A STENCIL TO MAKE A DOG CALLIGRAMME,
AND I'VE USED FIDO, THE NAME OF MY DOG.

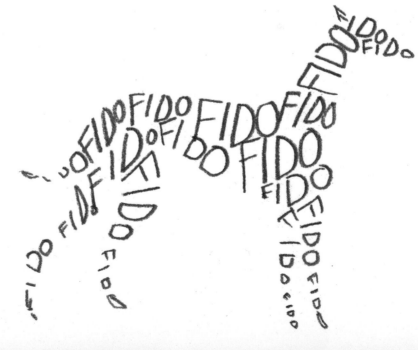

TRY YOUR OWN ON THIS OUTLINE.

YOU COULD ALSO TRY USING YOUR HAND.

TRACE AROUND YOUR HAND LIGHTLY WITH A PENCIL.
NOW WRITE ABOUT YOURSELF TO EITHER FILL THE SHAPE
OR WRITE AROUND THE OUTLINE.

EXQUISITE CORPSE

A SURREALIST ACTIVITY BASED ON AN OLD PARLOR GAME CALLED CONSEQUENCES.

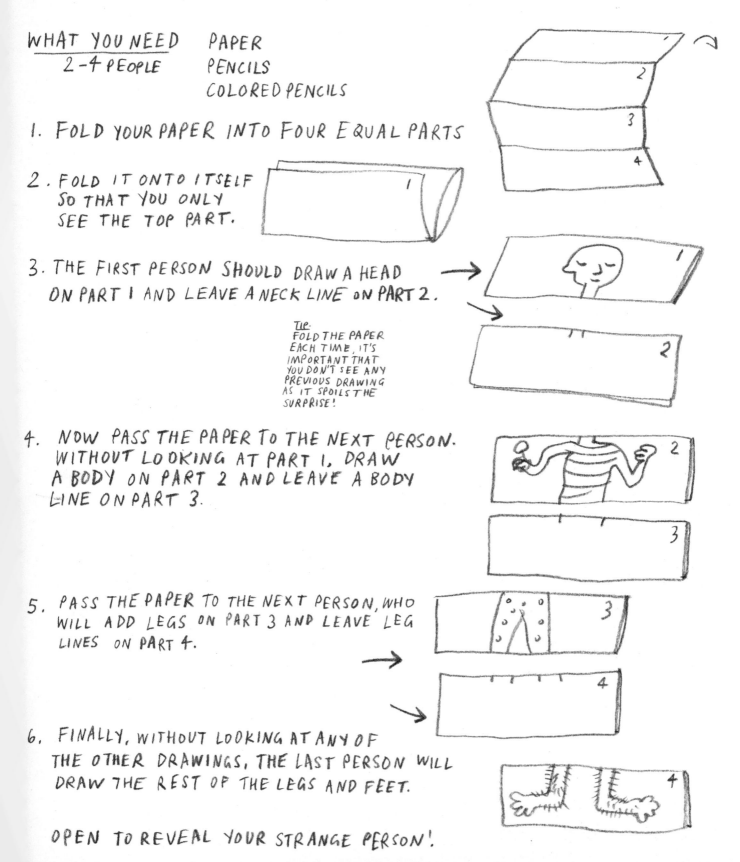

WHAT YOU NEED
2-4 PEOPLE

PAPER
PENCILS
COLORED PENCILS

1. FOLD YOUR PAPER INTO FOUR EQUAL PARTS

2. FOLD IT ONTO ITSELF SO THAT YOU ONLY SEE THE TOP PART.

3. THE FIRST PERSON SHOULD DRAW A HEAD ON PART 1 AND LEAVE A NECK LINE ON PART 2.

TIP:
FOLD THE PAPER EACH TIME, IT'S IMPORTANT THAT YOU DON'T SEE ANY PREVIOUS DRAWING AS IT SPOILS THE SURPRISE!

4. NOW PASS THE PAPER TO THE NEXT PERSON. WITHOUT LOOKING AT PART 1, DRAW A BODY ON PART 2 AND LEAVE A BODY LINE ON PART 3.

5. PASS THE PAPER TO THE NEXT PERSON, WHO WILL ADD LEGS ON PART 3 AND LEAVE LEG LINES ON PART 4.

6. FINALLY, WITHOUT LOOKING AT ANY OF THE OTHER DRAWINGS, THE LAST PERSON WILL DRAW THE REST OF THE LEGS AND FEET.

OPEN TO REVEAL YOUR STRANGE PERSON!

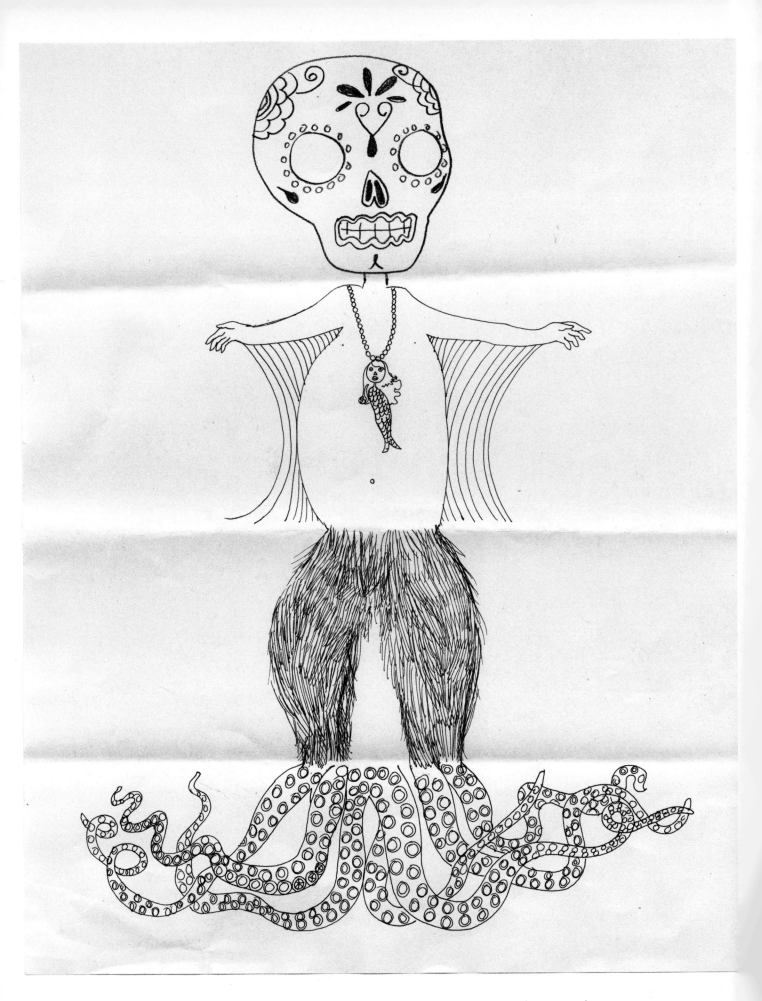

YOU CAN DO VARIATIONS WITH DIFFERENT SUBJECTS OR THEMES. TRY ANIMALS,
MYTHICAL CREATURES, AND OBJECTS. YOU CAN ALSO VARY HOW YOU FOLD THE PAPER.

ENTOPIC GRAPHOMANIA

A **SURREALIST** METHOD OF DRAWING IN WHICH DOTS ARE MADE ON THE GRAIN OF THE PAPER (THE LITTLE MARKS OR FLECKS YOU SEE IN THE TEXTURE OF THE PAPER).

ONCE YOU HAVE DRAWN THE DOTS, CONNECT THEM WITH EITHER CURVED OR STRAIGHT LINES.

NOW YOU TRY IT ON THIS TEXTURED PAPER. →

DECALCOMANIA

ACCIDENTAL BLOTS WERE USED BY THE SURREALISTS AS A STARTING POINT FOR SOME INCREDIBLE ART.

MAKE YOUR OWN INK BLOTS BY DROPPING INK OR WATERY PAINT ON BLANK PAPER. FOLD THE PAPER TO REPEAT THE SHAPE, OR BLOT (PRESS) WITH ANOTHER SHEET OF PAPER TO SPREAD INTO A RANDOM MARK.

ONCE DRY, TURN IT INTO WHATEVER THE SHAPE MAKES YOU THINK OF.

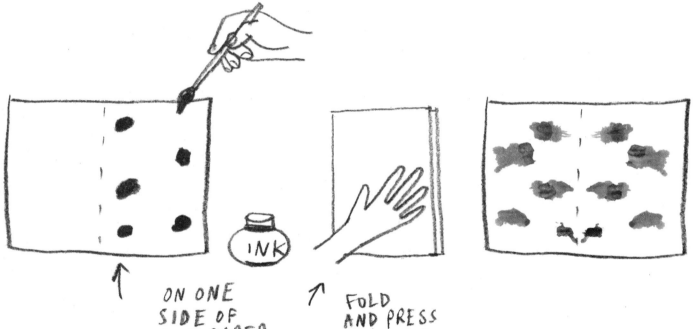

ON ONE SIDE OF THE PAPER

FOLD AND PRESS DOWN TO BLOT INK.

WHAT CAN YOU TURN THESE
ACCIDENTAL SHAPES INTO?

WHAT CAN YOU TURN THESE ACCIDENTAL SHAPES INTO?

Wassily Kandinsky

IT IS SAID KANDINSKY HAD A SPECIAL GIFT (called synaesthesia) THAT ENABLED HIM TO SEE SOUNDS AND HEAR COLOR. HE TRIED TO CREATE THE PAINTERLY EQUIVALENT OF A SYMPHONY THAT WOULD STIMULATE NOT JUST YOUR EYES BUT YOUR EARS AS WELL! HE MADE PAINTINGS USING SIMPLE ABSTRACT SHAPES LIKE THE CIRCLE, SQUARE, AND TRIANGLE, AND HE IS KNOWN AS THE FIRST ABSTRACT ARTIST. I'VE TRIED TO THINK OF THE LANGUAGE OF MUSICAL NOTES AS A SPECTRUM OF COLORS AND SHAPES FOR MY KANDINSKY-INSPIRED PAINTING HERE.

ART AND MUSIC

KANDINSKY COMPARED ART TO MUSIC. SOME OF HIS PAINTINGS AND SHAPES EVEN LOOK LIKE MUSICAL NOTATION, THE WAY THEY "DANCE" AROUND THE IMAGE.

HERE ARE SOME OF THE SHAPES I MADE IN RESPONSE TO THE SOUNDS I HEAR IN MY FAVORITE SONG.

KEYBOARD

ELECTRIC GUITAR

TAMBOURINE

WOMAN'S HIGH VOICE

FLUTE

DRUM BEAT

MAN'S VOICE

CHOOSE A SONG YOU LIKE AND TRY TO DRAW SOME SHAPES THAT YOU THINK SUIT THE MUSIC.
ARE THE NOTES SHORT? LONG? FAST? SLOW? DRAMATIC? HAPPY? SAD? DON'T THINK ABOUT THE SHAPES TOO MUCH. JUST RESPOND WITH YOUR PENCIL TO WHAT YOU HEAR.

ART AND MUSIC

"I applied STREAKS and BLOBS of COLORS onto the canvas ... and I made them SING with all the intensity I could."

Wassily Kandinsky

DRAW SOME MORE SHAPES TO MUSIC.

COLOR IN THESE SHAPES IN BRIGHT COLORS.

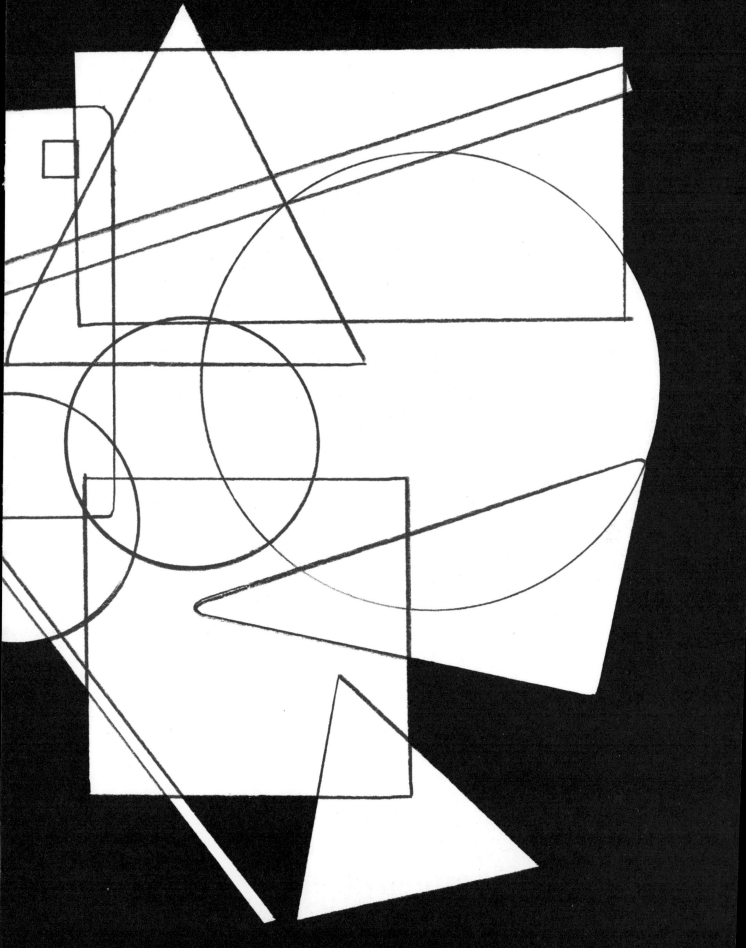

Henri Matisse

HENRI MATISSE IS ONE OF THE MOST FAMOUS ARTISTS IN THE WORLD. HE
NOT ONLY PAINTED WITH BRUSHES BUT HE ALSO MADE PICTURES FROM
CUT OUT PAPER AND CALLED IT "PAINTING WITH SCISSORS." THE
COMPOSITIONS WERE SOMETIMES ABSTRACT, BUT THE SHAPES REMIND US
OF THINGS LIKE PLANTS, PEOPLE, LANDSCAPES, AND ANIMALS. HERE I'VE
CREATED A CUT PAPER UNDERWATER LANDSCAPE. THE SHAPES AT FIRST
LOOK ABSTRACT, BUT ON CLOSER INSPECTION ARE A BIT LIKE FISH AND
PLANTS YOU MIGHT FIND UNDER THE SEA.

PAINTING with SCISSORS

USE SCISSORS  TO "DRAW"

MATISSE USED SCISSORS LIKE A PENCIL BUT INSTEAD OF DRAWING, HE CUT SHAPES OUT OF COLORED PAPER AND STUCK THEM DOWN TO MAKE HIS PICTURES. TAKE SOME SHEETS OF COLORED PAPER AND CUT OUT SOME SHAPES. HERE ARE SOME TO INSPIRE YOU. DON'T THINK TOO MUCH ABOUT WHAT YOU ARE DOING, JUST ENJOY THE PROCESS OF CUTTING, MOVING YOUR HAND AND ARM IN DIFFERENT DIRECTIONS. ONCE YOU HAVE CUT MANY RANDOM SHAPES, TRY TO ARRANGE THEM ON A PIECE OF LARGER PAPER (WHITE OR COLORED). USE THE PAGES HERE TO EXPERIMENT.

MATISSE USED SHAPES ↗
LIKE THESE BUT ALSO
STARS, PEOPLE, ANIMALS,
LETTERS.

YOU CAN USE THE PAPER
LEFTOVER SHAPES
TOO!

TRY STICKING
YOUR SHAPES
HERE ⟶

MAKE YOUR OWN COLORED PAPER BY PAINTING WHITE PAPER WITH GOUACHE OR POSTER PAINT. ONCE DRY YOU CAN USE IT TO MAKE CUT PAPER ART. TRY TO ORGANIZE THE SHAPES INTO A PICTURE OF YOUR HOME, YOUR FAMILY, SEASIDE, OR PARK.

✳ Handy Tip: Paint the edges of the paper too OR USE CLOTH instead of paper.

TRY STICKING YOUR SHAPES HERE.

A GARDEN

THE SEA

MATISSE MADE A FAMOUS PICTURE CALLED "THE SNAIL." IT IS MADE OF
CUT-UP SQUARES ARRANGED IN A FULL CIRCLE. IT DOES NOT LOOK LIKE
A "REAL" SNAIL, BUT THE SHAPES REMIND US OF THE SHAPE OF A SNAIL.

HERE IS
A BIRD

TRY TO MAKE YOUR ABSTRACT SHAPES REMIND YOU OF SOMETHING—
PERHAPS A BIRD, A FACE, OR AN ANIMAL.

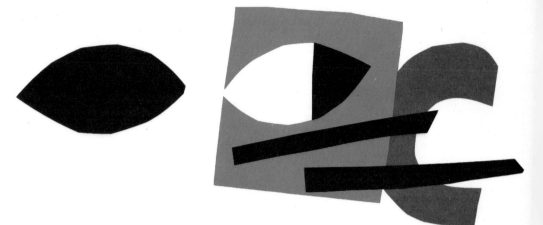

MATISSE MADE MANY CUT PAPER IMAGES FOR A BOOK
CALLED JAZZ. ITS THEME IS CIRCUS AND THEATER.

CAN YOU MAKE A CUT PAPER IMAGE OR A DRAWING BASED ON
THESE TITLES THAT COME FROM THE BOOK?
USE VIBRANT COLORS LIKE RED, YELLOW, ORANGE. BLUE, PURPLE, GREEN,
and BLACK.

THE SWORD-SWALLOWER

THE HORSE, the RIDER, and THE CLOWN

Ben Nicholson

BEN NICHOLSON'S ART WAS INSPIRED BY AN OLD FISHERMAN CALLED ALFRED WALLIS WHOM HE MET IN THE SEASIDE TOWN OF ST. IVES. WALLIS HAD NEVER BEEN TO ART SCHOOL AND PAINTED IN A PRIMITIVE WAY WITH HOUSE PAINTS AND BITS OF OLD CARDBOARD. NICHOLSON USED THESE MATERIALS IN HIS WORK BUT MADE HIS ART "MODERN" USING GEOMETRIC SHAPES LIKE THE STYLES OF THE ARTISTS PICASSO AND BRAQUE. HERE I'VE COPIED HOW NICHOLSON WOULD MAKE A "RELIEF" SCULPTURE OUT OF SIMPLE SHAPES AND CARDBOARD.

* To create a painting in RELIEF is to give the impression that the material has been raised above the background plane.

CUBIST-INSPIRED STILL LIFE

NICHOLSON WAS INSPIRED BY PICASSO AND CUBISM. HE MADE MANY STILL LIFES USING THE FOLLOWING TECHNIQUE.

WHAT YOU NEED

PAPER
PENCILS
CRAYONS OR PAINTS

* CUBISM
AN ART MOVEMENT STARTED BY PICASSO AND BRAQUE WHERE THEY TRIED TO SHOW A SUBJECT FROM ALL DIFFERENT ANGLES IN ONE PICTURE.

1. DRAW SOME JUGS, CUPS, OR VASES.

2. NOW DRAW SOME RECTANGLES, SOME AT ANGLES, ON TOP OF YOUR DRAWING.

3. NOW COLOR IN, IGNORING THE REALISTIC SHAPES OF THE JUGS, AND CHANGE COLOR OR TONE WHERE THE RECTANGLES HAVE MADE NEW SHAPES.

DRAW SOME SIMPLE OBJECTS YOU SEE ON YOUR TABLE OR THAT YOU CAN
FIND. NOW, COPYING THE INSTRUCTIONS ON THE PREVIOUS PAGE, TRY TO
CREATE A CUBIST-STYLE STILL LIFE.

CARDBOARD RELIEF

NICHOLSON MADE MANY PICTURES USING SIMPLE SHAPES MADE OUT OF OLD BITS OF CARDBOARD.

WHAT YOU NEED

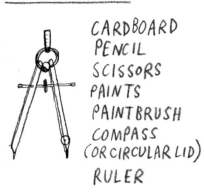

CARDBOARD
PENCIL
SCISSORS
PAINTS
PAINTBRUSH
COMPASS
(OR CIRCULAR LID)
RULER

1. CUT A RECTANGLE OF CARDBOARD TO WORK ON.
2. CUT SOME CARDBOARD CIRCLES, RECTANGLES, AND SQUARES.
3. ARRANGE THEM ON THE BACKGROUND UNTIL YOU ARE HAPPY WITH THE COMPOSITION.
4. ONCE DRY, PAINT WHITE.
   YOU MAY NEED SEVERAL COATS OF WHITE PAINT.

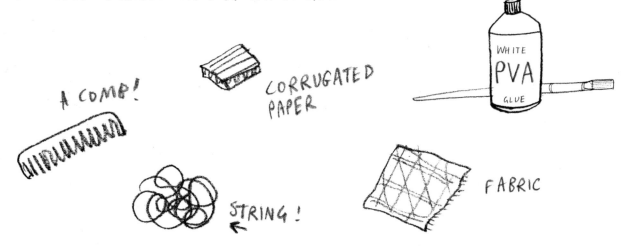

A COMB!

CORRUGATED PAPER

WHITE PVA GLUE

STRING!

FABRIC

5. ONCE YOU HAVE MADE YOUR FIRST RELIEF, EXPERIMENT FURTHER WITH DIFFERENT THICKNESSES OF CARDBOARD. YOU CAN ALSO STICK DOWN PIECES OF FABRIC, OR ANYTHING YOU CAN GLUE TO THE CARDBOARD.
6. PAINT OVER EVERYTHING IN WHITE. YOU MAY NEED SEVERAL COATS OF PAINT. IT WILL NOW LOOK MORE LIKE A SCULPTURE (OR RELIEF) AS THE WHITE PAINT MAKES EVERYTHING COME TOGETHER. IT ALSO EMPHASIZES THE SHADOWS. YOU CAN ADD COLOR ONCE THE WHITE PAINT IS DRY.

* A RELIEF IS A DESIGN OR SCULPTURE RAISED FROM A FLAT BACKGROUND TO GIVE A 3-D EFFECT.

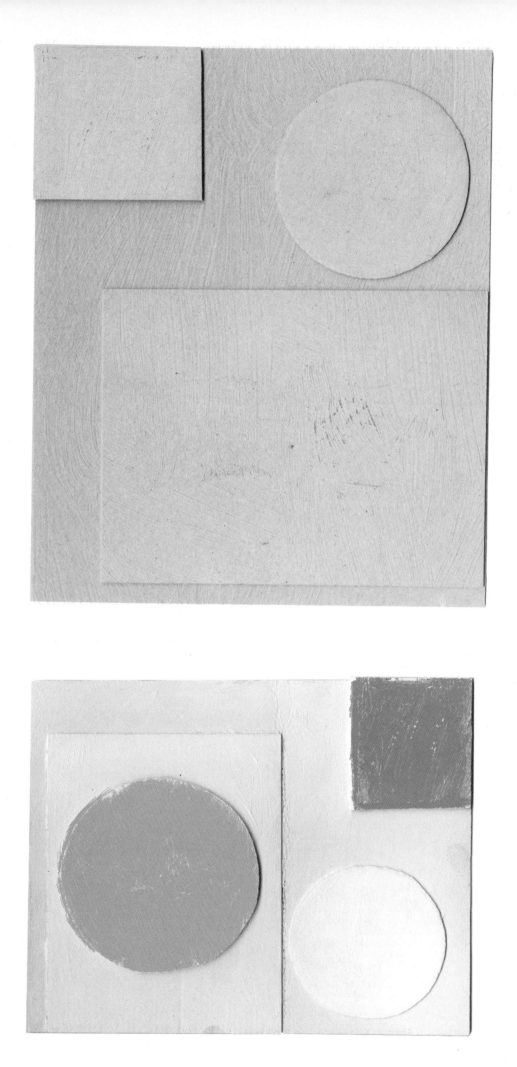

Frida Kahlo

FRIDA KAHLO WAS A MEXICAN ARTIST WHO STARTED PAINTING AS A
TEENAGER. HER PAINTINGS AND DRAWINGS ARE ALL ABOUT HER LIFE,
DREAMS, AND FEARS. SHE LOVED THE **VIBRANT** COLORS OF HER COUNTRY
AND LIKED TO ADD HER PETS AND DECORATIVE FRAMES TO HER PAINTINGS.
ONE IMPORTANT THING THAT FRIDA UNDERSTOOD WAS THAT WHEN LOOKING
FOR SOMETHING TO DRAW WE CAN START BY DRAWING OURSELVES.

DRAW OR PAINT YOUR SELF-PORTRAIT.

SELF-PORTRAIT

IN HER SELF-PORTRAITS FRIDA KAHLO EXAGGERATED CERTAIN FEATURES, LIKE JOINING HER EYEBROWS AND PAINTING A MUSTACHE, A BIT LIKE A CARICATURE OF HERSELF.

TRY TO IDENTIFY A SPECIAL FEATURE OF YOUR FACE AND DRAW IT IN AN EXAGGERATED WAY.

DRAW OR PAINT YOUR PORTRAIT IN THE SPACE, AND ADD SOME THINGS YOU ARE INTERESTED IN. FRIDA USED TO DRAW HER PET MONKEY OR PARROT.

"THE FLYING BED"

IN THE PAINTING "THE FLYING BED," FRIDA
PAINTED HERSELF LYING IN BED IN HOSPITAL,
WITH THINGS THAT UPSET HER FLYING
AROUND THE BED.

IMAGINE THIS IS YOUR BED; YOU ARE LYING
ON IT AND DREAMING OR THINKING. DRAW YOURSELF
AND WHAT YOU SEE OR IMAGINE IN THE SPACE
AROUND THE BED.

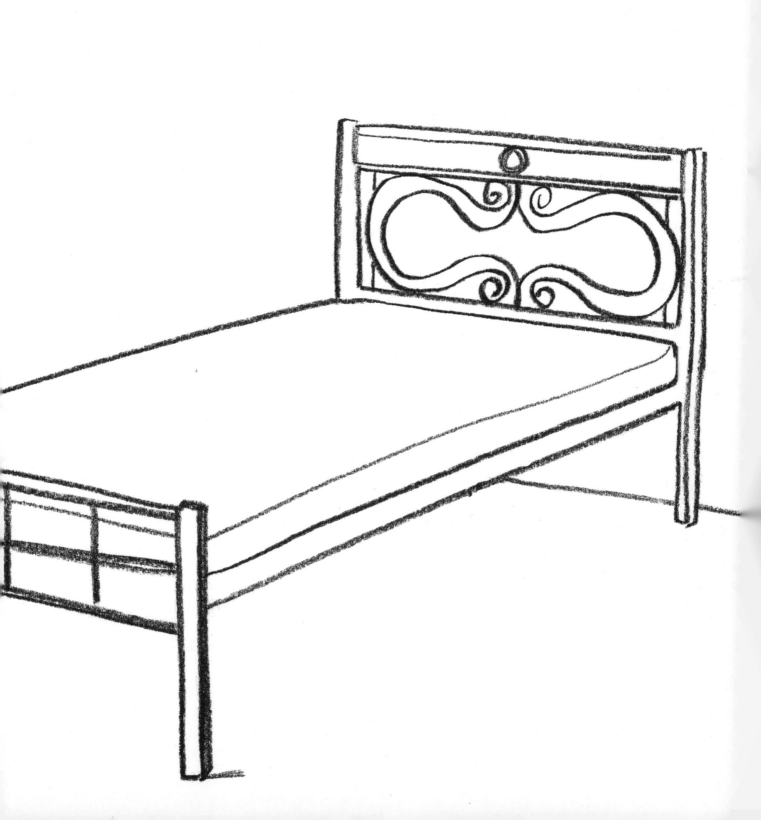

FRIDA KAHLO WAS INFLUENCED BY MEXICAN
CULTURE AND MYTHOLOGY. SHE OFTEN INCLUDED
THE MONKEY, WHICH WAS USUALLY PORTRAYED
AS A SIGN OF BADNESS—BUT SHE PAINTED IT AS
A TENDER AND PROTECTIVE FIGURE.
OTHER INFLUENCES INCLUDE HER
PETS, SUCH AS MONKEYS, DOGS,
CATS, AND PARROTS.

COLOR IN THIS MONKEY

MEXICAN GLYPHS

YEAR

I DAY

SUN

SKY

PERSON

SNAKE

ROAD

JAGUAR

BONE

TO SCATTER

WOMAN

BOOK

TO GRAB

CLOUD

EARTH, LAND

TWENTY

HOUSE

WATER

ANCIENT MAYAN (MEXICAN) WRITING DID NOT USE LETTERS TO SPELL WORDS, BUT GLYPHS (hieroglyphic characters or symbols).

SOME GLYPHS REPRESENTED SYLLABLES AND SOME STOOD FOR THE WHOLE WORD.

TRY TO MAKE YOUR OWN GLYPHS IN THE GRID. THEY DON'T HAVE TO LOOK exactly LiKE THE OBJECT BUT SHOULD MAKE YOU THINK OF IT WHEN YOU SEE IT.

USE THEM TO MAKE UP A STORY. HERE'S MINE. . .

1 DAY A WOMAN LOOKED UP AT THE SKY AND SAW A CLOUD. IT WAS IN THE SHAPE OF A JAGUAR. FRIGHTENED BY IT, SHE RAN DOWN THE ROAD BACK TO HER HOUSE.

Jasper Johns

JASPER JOHNS USES VERY SIMPLE IMAGES AND SYMBOLS THAT HAVE STRONG MEANINGS, LIKE TARGETS, FLAGS, NUMBERS, AND LETTERS. HIS MOST FAMOUS PAINTING IS OF THE AMERICAN FLAG, WHICH HE PAINTED AFTER HAVING A DREAM ABOUT IT. WHAT I LIKE ABOUT HIS WORK IS THE WAY HE TAKES ONE THING, LIKE THE FLAG, AND MAKES MANY DIFFERENT VERSIONS OF IT USING LAYERS OF COLOR AND TEXTURES SO THAT IT BECOMES SOMETHING QUITE DIFFERENT. IN MY TARGET IMAGE, I KEPT CHANGING THE COLORS UNTIL I FOUND THIS COMBINATION.

MAKE A TEXTURED TARGET PAINTING like JASPER JOHNS'

WHAT YOU NEED

Old newspaper
PVA glue
Brushes
Paint (acrylic)

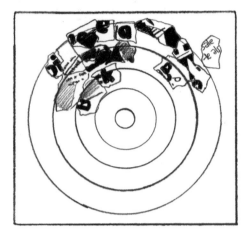

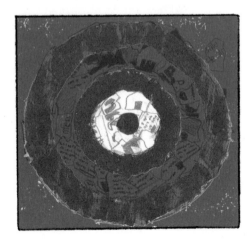

1. RIP UP THE NEWSPAPER INTO LITTLE PIECES. GLUE ONTO TARGET SHAPE OPPOSITE.

2. USE THE GLUE ON BOTH SIDES OF THE NEWSPAPER.

3. ONCE DRY, PAINT YOUR TARGET IN BRIGHT COLORS.

4. USE LOTS OF THICK PAINT TO COVER THE NEWSPRINT. YOU SHOULD SEE ITS TEXTURE.

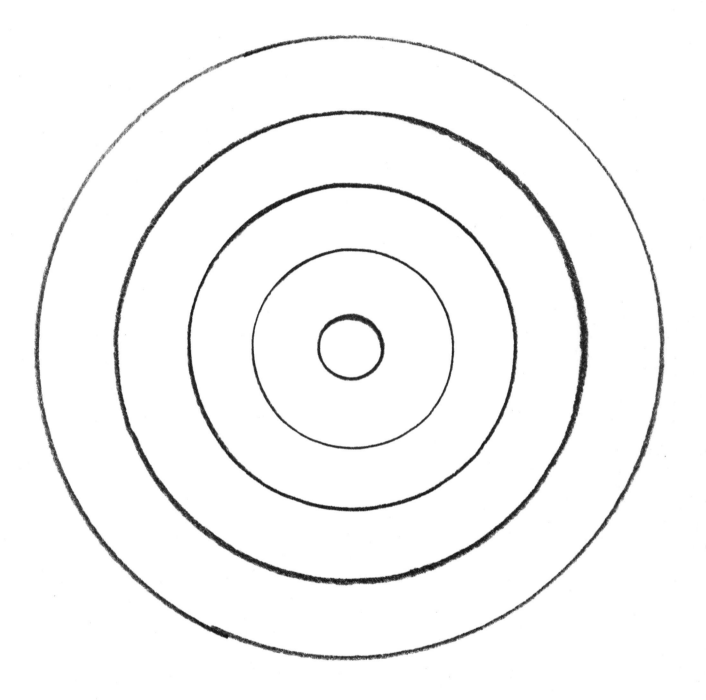

COLOR IN THE LETTERS AND
NUMBERS, MAKING EACH ONE
DIFFERENT.

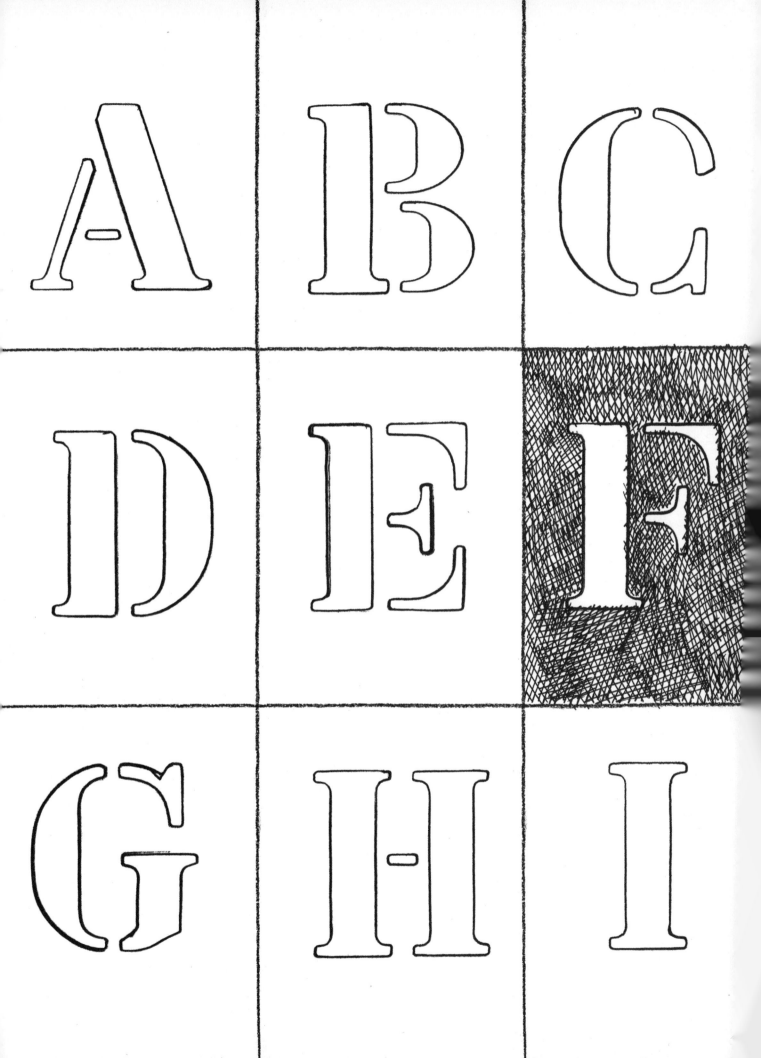

DRAW OR STENCIL
YOUR OWN NUMBERS
OR LETTERS AND
COLOR THEM IN.

USING STENCIL LETTERS OR NUMBERS, PLACE ONE ON TOP OF ANOTHER TO CREATE A PATTERN. YOU CAN ALSO USE HAND-DRAWN LETTERS.

TRY WRITING YOUR OWN NAME IN THIS STYLE.

COLOR IN THESE SHAPES.

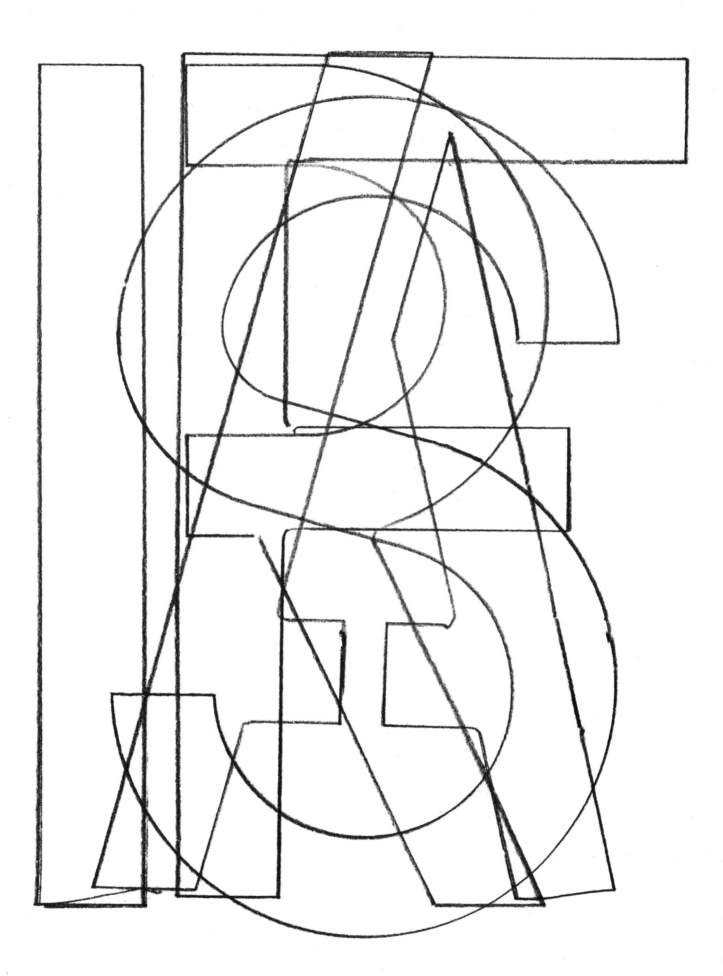

Paul Klee

PAUL KLEE WAS AMBIDEXTROUS: HE WROTE WITH HIS RIGHT HAND AND
PAINTED WITH HIS LEFT. MANY OF HIS DRAWINGS AND PAINTINGS
LOOK LIKE LINES STACKING UP ON TOP OF EACH OTHER IN PLAYFUL
DOODLES. HE USED BRIGHT COLORS AND MADE INTRICATE PATTERNS.
MANY OF THEM REMIND ME OF crayon etching. HERE I'VE
SCRAPED A LINEAR "STACKING" PATTERN TO MAKE A
KLEE-LIKE DOODLE.

CRAYON ETCHING

KLEE MADE ALL KINDS OF LINES IN HIS WORK. SOME OF THEM LOOKED AS THOUGH THEY WERE "SCRATCHED OUT" OF THE PAINT. YOU CAN MAKE SIMILAR KINDS OF MARKS BY SCRATCHING LINES OUT OF PAINT-COVERED WAX. IT IS CALLED "SCRATCH ART" OR "CRAYON ETCHING." IT IS VERY SIMPLE TO DO.

WHAT YOU NEED

WHITE CARD
WAX CRAYONS (BRIGHT COLORS)
BLACK GOUACHE OR ACRYLIC PAINT
WIDE, FLAT BRUSH
2H PENCIL OR COCKTAIL STICK OR SHARP TOOL
PAPER TOWEL

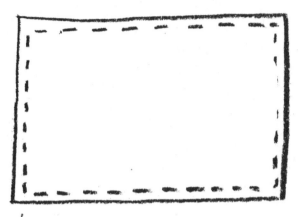

1. DRAW A BORDER ON WHITE CARD.

2. RUB WAX CRAYONS ONTO PAPER, UP TO YOUR BORDER, LEAVING NO WHITE SPACES. RUB AWAY SURPLUS WAX WITH PAPER TOWEL.

3. PAINT OVER WAX CRAYON WITH BLACK ACRYLIC OR GOUACHE PAINT WITH A WIDE, FLAT BRUSH. COVER EVENLY. PAINT SHOULD BE QUITE THICK BUT NOT LUMPY.

4. SCRAPE YOUR PATTERN INTO THE BLACK PAINT TO REVEAL THE WAX COLORS. RUB AWAY SURPLUS DRIED PAINT.

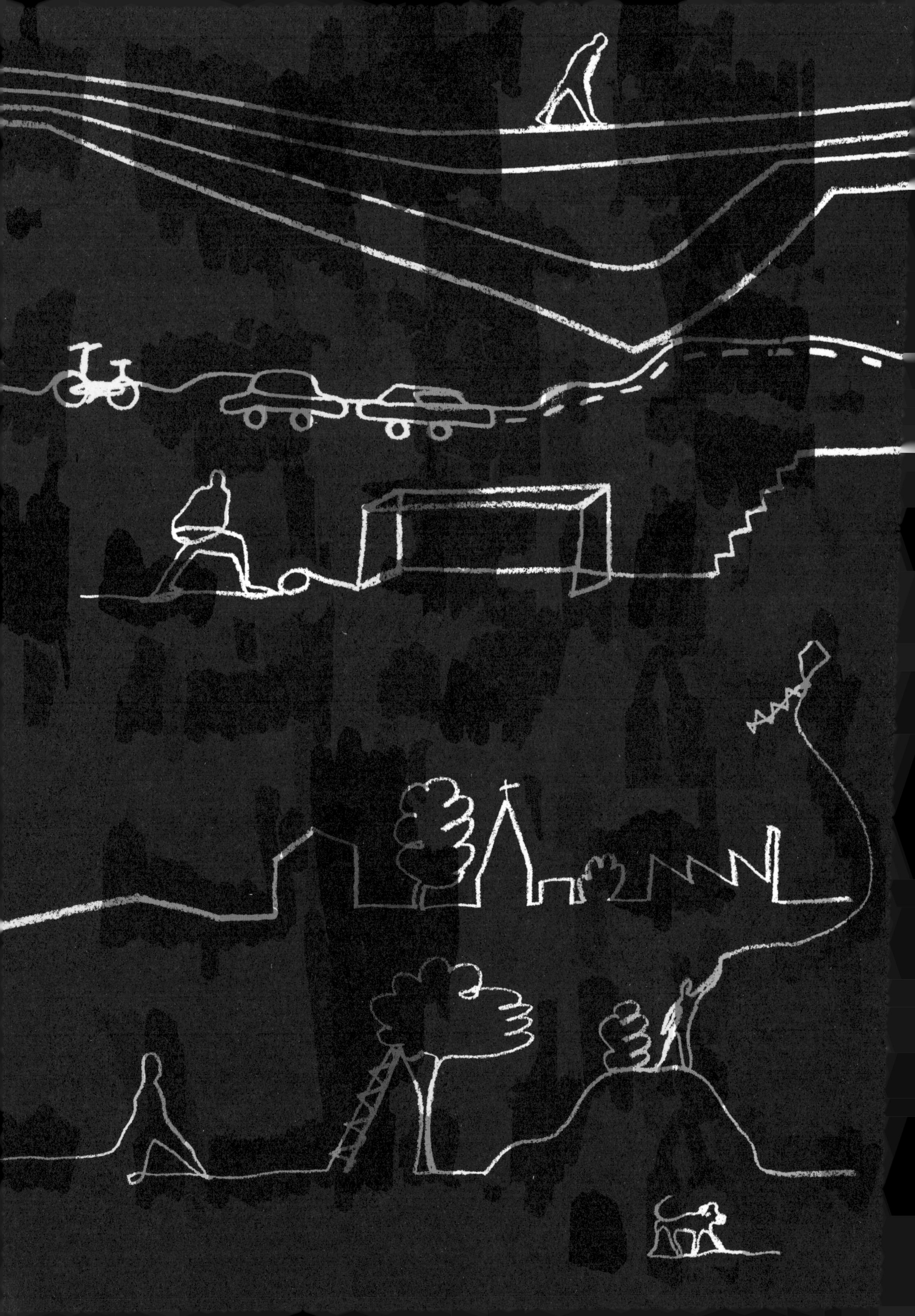

KLEE LIKED TO INSERT SHAPES INTO LINES.
TRY AND DRAW SOME SIMPLE OBJECTS OR SHAPES
ONTO THESE LINES.

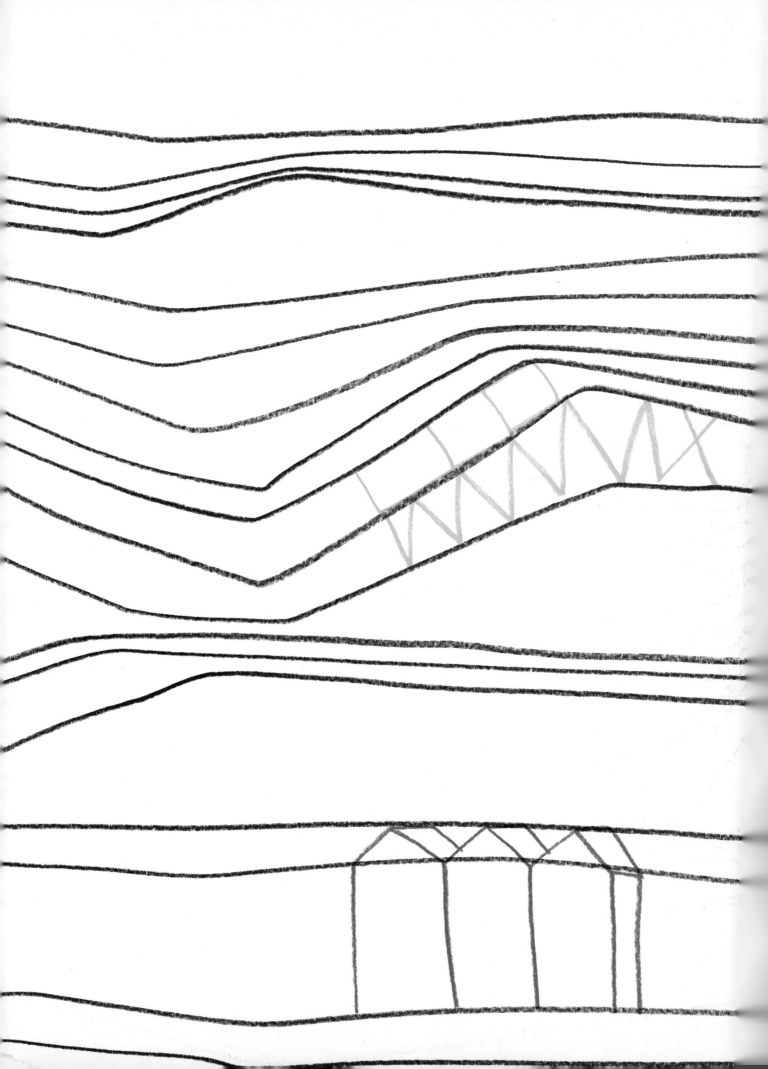

PAUL KLEE WAS A MASTER OF COLOR. USING BRIGHT
WATERCOLOR OR OIL PASTELS, COLOR IN THE SHAPES
OPPOSITE.
BELOW, DRAW YOUR OWN STACKING SHAPES.
BUILD THEM UP, PIECE BY PIECE, LIKE DOODLING,
THEN COLOR IN.

CONTINUOUS LINE

PAUL KLEE WAS KNOWN FOR "TAKING A LINE FOR A WALK."
TRY TO TAKE YOUR PENCIL ON A CONTINUOUS LINE WALK.
TRY NOT TO TAKE YOUR PENCIL OFF THE PAPER.
DRAW ALL THE DIFFERENT THINGS YOU MIGHT SEE ON A
WALK IN YOUR TOWN OR CITY.

Emily Kngwarreye

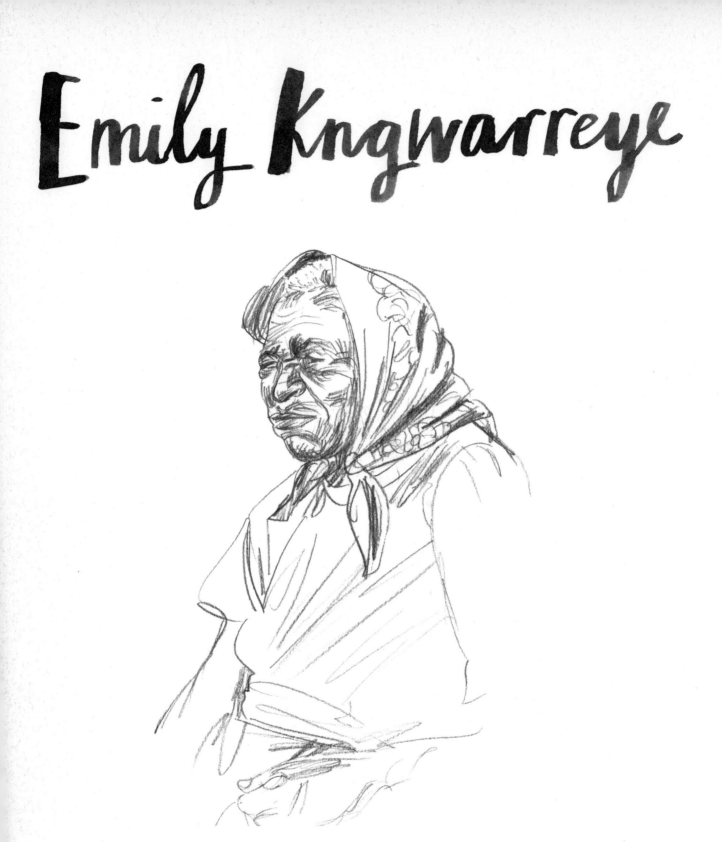

EMILY KNGWARREYE WAS ONE OF THE MOST FAMOUS AND SUCCESSFUL INDIGENOUS AUSTRALIAN ARTISTS. SHE DID NOT START PAINTING SERIOUSLY UNTIL SHE WAS EIGHTY YEARS OLD. AND SHE DEVELOPED HER OWN STYLE BASED ON THE ABORIGINAL TRADITION OF DOTS AND LINES. SOME OF HER BIG DOT PAINTINGS WERE MADE WITH A SHAVING BRUSH— SHE CALLED IT HER "DUMP DUMP" STYLE. I'VE MADE A PAINTING HERE USING THE END OF MY BRUSH DIPPED IN PAINT.

Aboriginal Symbols

INDIGENOUS AUSTRALIAN ART IS BASED ON IMPORTANT ANCIENT STORIES PASSED DOWN THROUGH HUNDREDS OF GENERATIONS, CALLED "DREAMTIME." ABORIGINAL ARTISTS USE A SET OF SYMBOLS IN THEIR PAINTINGS TO TELL STORIES OR DREAMS ABOUT THEIR HISTORY AND CULTURE.

stars

rain

clouds

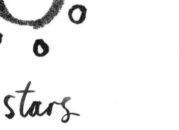

water, rainbow

campsite stone, well, fire, or hole

flowers or fruit

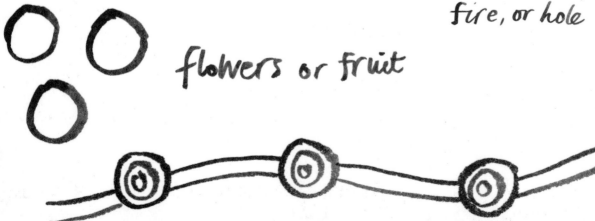

two men sitting

forest

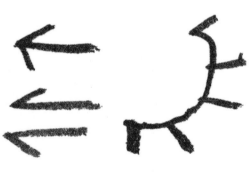

traveling sign with
circles as a resting place

fire or smoke,
water or blood

man

footprints

boomerang

digging
sticks

rainbow or
cloud or cliff

yam plant

long journey with waterholes

Aboriginal Symbols

MAKE UP YOUR OWN SYMBOLS TO REPRESENT YOUR TOWN OR CITY.

FOR EXAMPLE

PARK   HOUSE   BUS STOP

Emily did not only use dots in her paintings, she also used lines and painted YAM TRACKS.
They look like a bird's eye view of yam roots under the ground or the cracked earth. The yam plant is an important food for the Aborigines.

Mix up some watery paint and try to paint the roots of a tree or plant under the ground.

↙

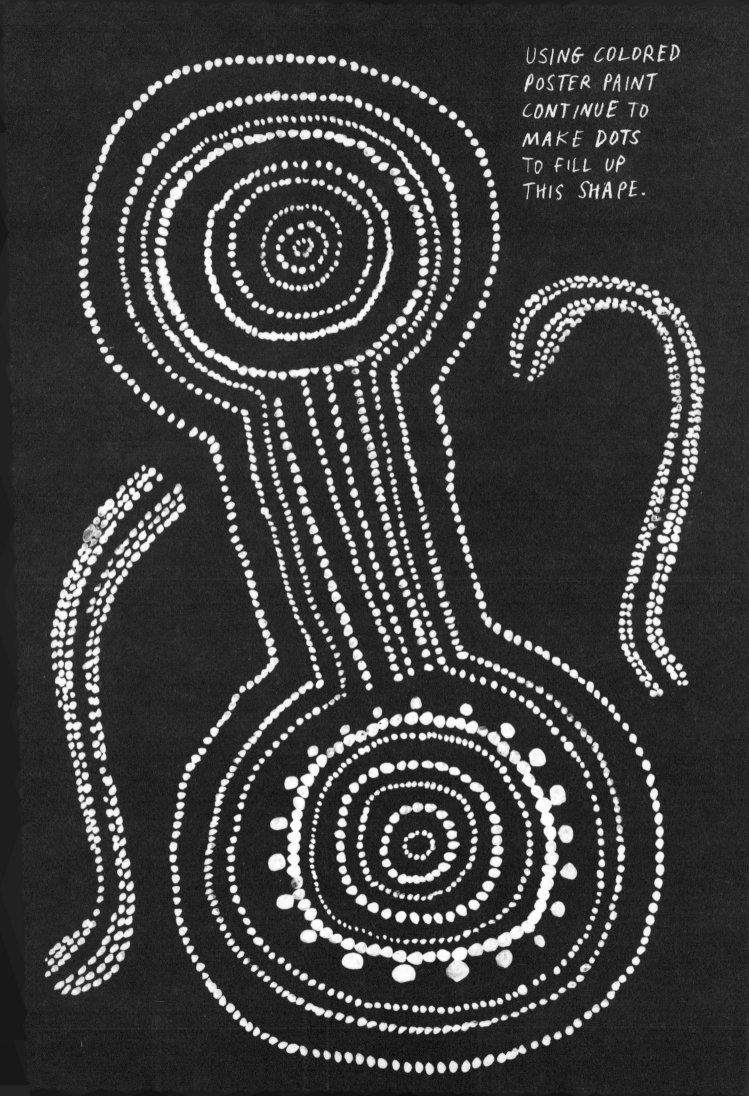

USING COLORED
POSTER PAINT
CONTINUE TO
MAKE DOTS
TO FILL UP
THIS SHAPE.

NOW MAKE
YOUR OWN
COLORFUL DOT
DESIGNS IN
THIS SHAPE.

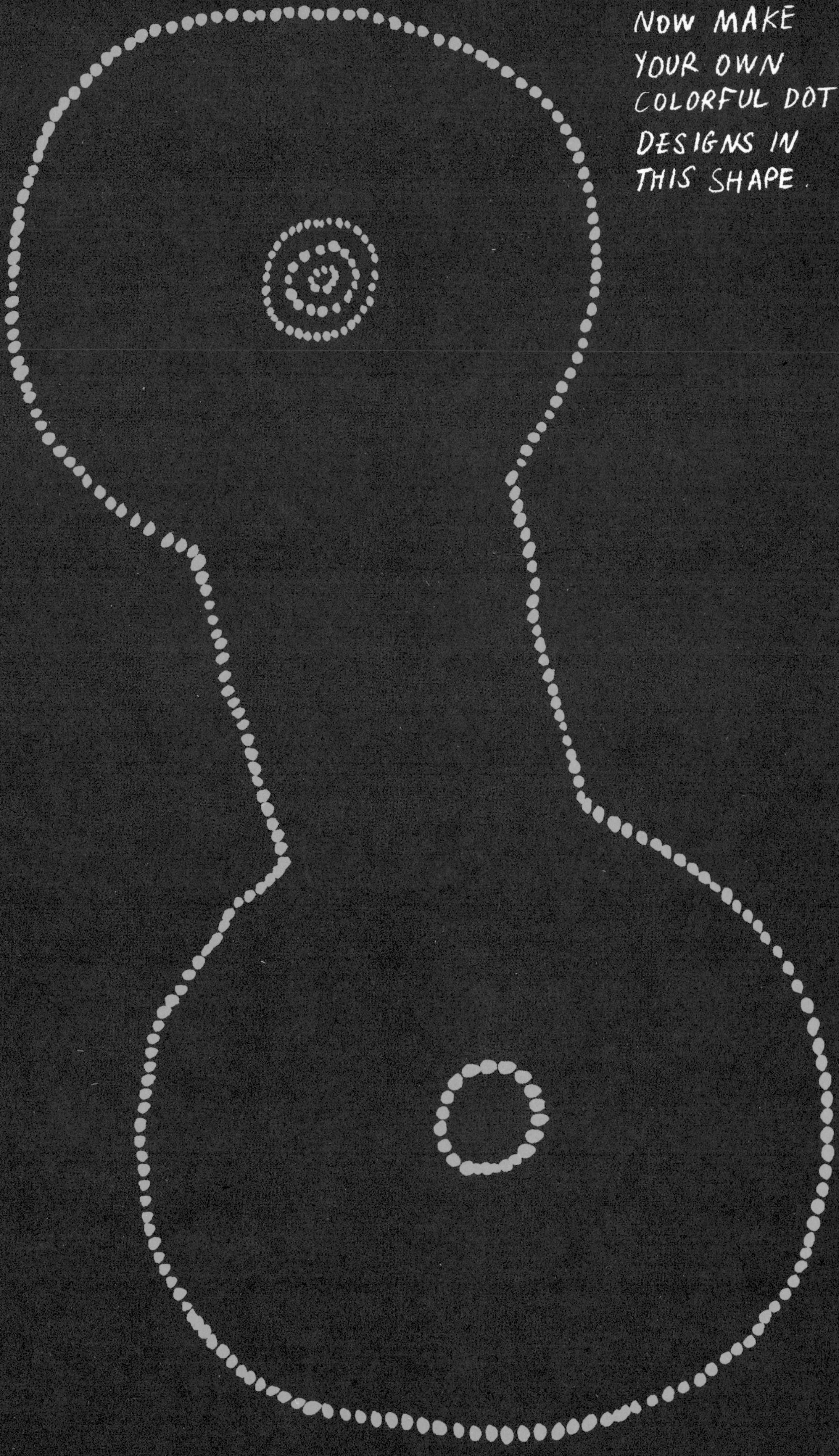

ABORIGINAL ART WAS ORIGINALLY DRAWN IN THE SAND, ON WALLS, ON BARK, AND ON BODIES. MUCH OF IT WAS MADE OF DOTS. DOTS WERE A CODE FOR SECRET INFORMATION.

PRACTICE MAKING PAINT DOT PATTERNS.

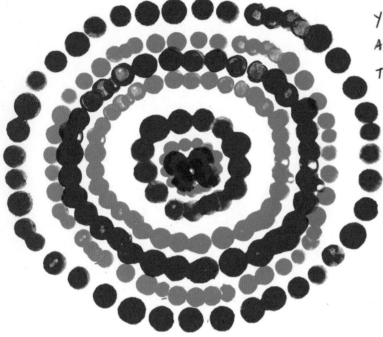

YOU CAN USE A FINE BRUSH,
A COTTON SWAB,
THE END OF A PENCIL (WITH ERASER TOP),
OR THE END OF A SMALL STICK
OR PAINTBRUSH.
THE PAINT SHOULD BE QUITE THICK,
NOT WATERY.

CLAP OR DIGGING STICKS

THESE ARE WOODEN STICKS SHARPENED AT THE END AND USED BY THE ABORIGINES TO DIG FOR ROOTS, ANTS, OR SMALL REPTILES. THEY ARE ALSO AN ANCIENT MUSICAL INSTRUMENT USED IN CEREMONIES. YOU "CLAP" THEM TOGETHER TO MAKE A SOUND.

MAKE YOUR OWN CLAPSTICK.

WHAT YOU NEED

STICKS approx 6-8 in. long
(DOWEL, OR OLD BROOMSTICK)
COTTON SWABS OR FINE BRUSH
ACRYLIC PAINTS
BRUSHES
SANDPAPER

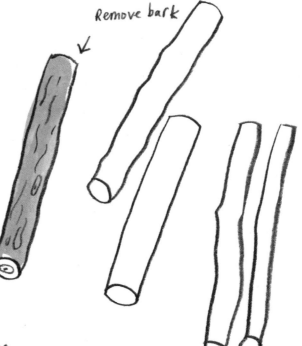

Remove bark

1. REMOVE THE BARK IF YOU CAN OR PAINT ON TOP OF THE BARK.

2. LIGHTLY SAND THE STICKS.

3. PAINT A BASE COAT COLOR ALL OVER THE STICK.

4. ONCE DRY, PAINT YOUR PATTERN, ONE COLOR AT A TIME.
   TO SPEED UP DRYING, USE A HAIR-DRYER.

YOU CAN PAINT A DOT PATTERN OR DOT SNAKES AND REPTILE SHAPES, OR USE SOME OF THE SYMBOLS SHOWN IN THIS BOOK.
MY FAVORITE PATTERN ON THE STICKS IS THE MULTICOLORED STRIPES.

*Handy Tip

USE A SMALL CARDBOARD BOX WITH HOLES PUNCHED IN TO MAKE A PAINTING/DRYING STAND.
OR USE A LUMP OF PLAY CLAY OR AN OLD CUP.

USE A LARGER BRUSH FOR THE BASE COLOR, AND FINE
BRUSHES OR COTTON SWABS FOR THE DOTS AND PATTERNS
OR STRIPES.

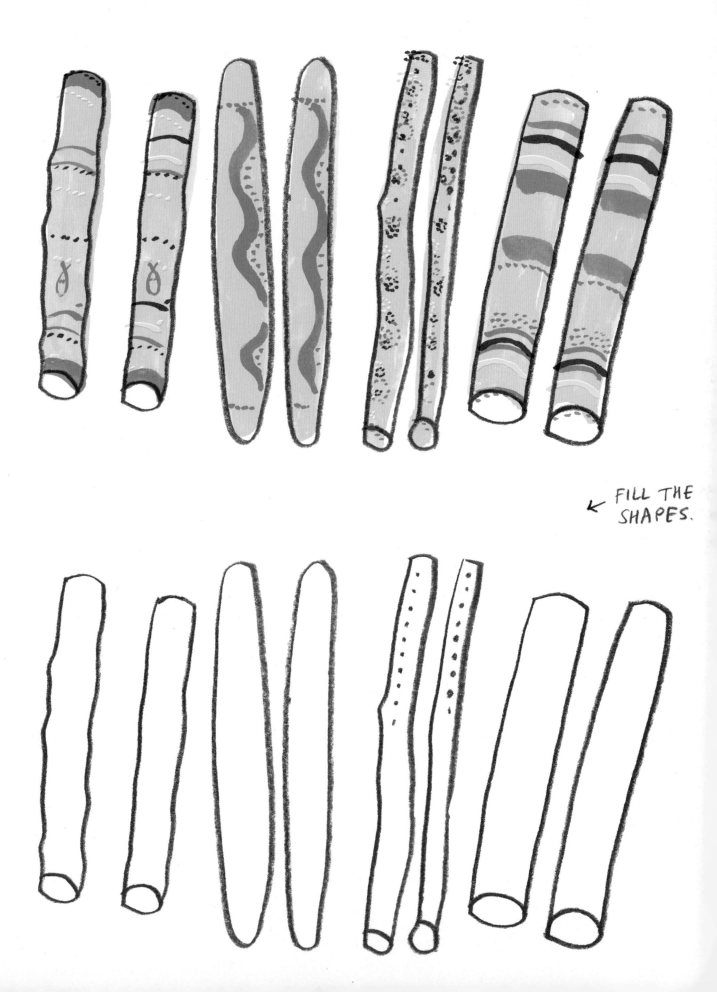

← FILL THE
SHAPES.

Andy Warhol

ANDY WARHOL'S PAINTINGS OFTEN IMITATED OLD-FASHIONED PRINTING, WHERE
THE COLOR NEVER QUITE FITS EXACTLY INSIDE THE BLACK OUTLINE. HE
MADE HUNDREDS OF IMAGES IN THIS WAY, OF EVERYDAY OBJECTS LIKE
SHOES, FOOD, AND HIS BELOVED CATS. HE GREW UP SURROUNDED BY
THEM. THEY WERE ALL CALLED SAM EXCEPT ONE CALLED HESTER.
HE EVEN MADE A COLORING BOOK ABOUT THEM CALLED "25 CATS NAMED
SAM AND ONE BLUE PUSSY." I'VE DRAWN MY CAT HERE USING WARHOL'S
DRAWING STYLE.

INK BLOTTING DRAWING (MONOPRINTING)

ANDY WARHOL USED THIS TECHNIQUE TO MAKE MANY OF HIS DRAWINGS. IT IS A BASIC FORM OF PRINTMAKING AND ALLOWS YOU TO MAKE "MULTIPLES" OF THE SAME DRAWING.

<u>WHAT YOU NEED</u>

ABSORBENT PAPER (CARTRIDGE, PHOTOCOPY PAPER)
NONABSORBENT PAPER (TRACING PAPER, PAPER PALETTE)
COLORED INKS OR WATERCOLOR
OLD FOUNTAIN PEN, FINE BRUSH, OR STICK

STICKY TAPE
PENCIL

NONABSORBENT (DRAWING SIDE)
ABSORBENT (PRINTING SIDE)

1. DRAW OR TRACE YOUR IMAGE IN PENCIL ON THE PAPER.

TAPE HINGE

2. JOIN (WITH TAPE) THE TWO PIECES OF PAPER TOGETHER SO THAT THEY CAN OPEN LIKE A BOOK.

INK

3. USE THE INK PEN TO DRAW A SMALL PART OF YOUR TRACED LINE.

RUB OR PRESS DOWN

4. BEFORE THE INK DRIES, PRESS DOWN ONTO THE ABSORBENT PAPER (like closing your book)

5. REPEAT STEPS 3-4 UNTIL DRAWING IS COMPLETE.

6. ONCE DRY, COLOR WITH COLOR INKS OR PENS.

BLACK LINE and
TRANSLUCENT COLOR

COLOR IN USING COLORED INKS, FELT-TIP PENS, OR WATERCOLOR PAINTS.

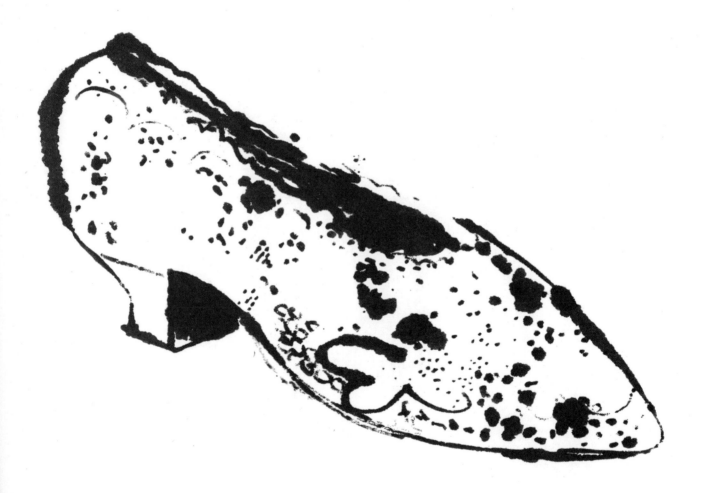

✳ Handy Tip

DON'T WORRY ABOUT BEING TOO NEAT! WHEN
YOU HAVE A STRONG BLACK LINE AND YOU USE
TRANSLUCENT COLOR, THE EFFECT OF
GOING "OVER THE LINES" LOOKS GOOD.

ANDY WARHOL MADE MANY IMAGES BASED ON MASS-PRODUCED IMAGES LIKE COCA-COLA
BOTTLES, CANS OF SOUP, AND FAMOUS PEOPLE.
YOU CAN MAKE YOUR OWN WARHOL-INSPIRED IMAGES BY PHOTOCOPYING AN IMAGE
(OR DRAWING) OF SOMETHING EVERYDAY OR A PORTRAIT OF YOURSELF OR A
FAMOUS PERSON.

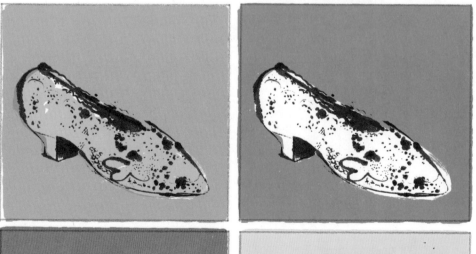

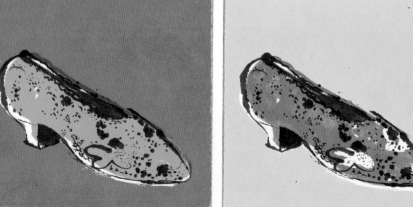

MULTIPLES

COLOR IN WITH
DIFFERENT COLORS

COPY A BLACK AND WHITE IMAGE AT LEAST FOUR TIMES AND
PASTE TOGETHER ON A SEPARATE SHEET OF PAPER. NOW COLOR
THEM IN, MAKING EACH DRAWING OR PHOTOCOPY A DIFFERENT COLOR.

MULTIPLES

DRAW OR STICK YOUR PHOTOCOPIES HERE,
THEN COLOR IN WITH FELT-TIP PENS,
CRAYONS, OR PAINT.

Andy Warhol Handwriting

Andy Warhol copied his mother's handwriting
using a dip pen and ink.
Try writing with a dip pen.
copy these letters.

a b c d e f g h i j

k l m n o p q r s t

u v w x y z

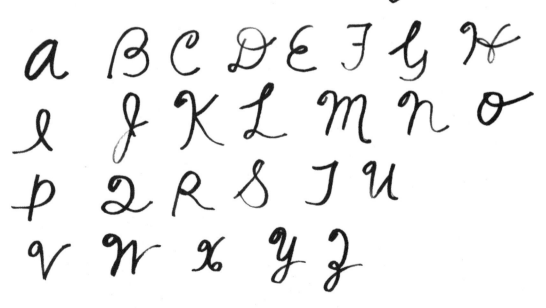

A B C D E F G H
I J K L M N O
P Q R S T U
V W X Y Z

a b c

INK

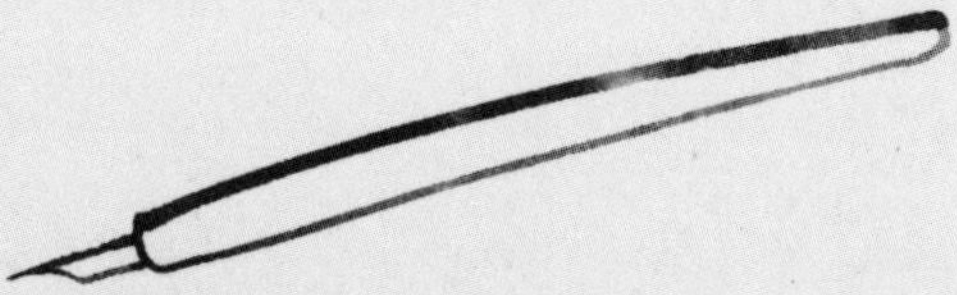

Dip pen or fountain pen.

Hannah Höch

HANNAH HÖCH WAS ONE OF THE FIRST ARTISTS TO CUT UP PHOTOGRAPHS AND STICK THEM TOGETHER IN A NEW WAY TO MAKE PHOTOMONTAGES. TO MAKE MY OWN KIND OF PHOTOMONTAGES, I HAVE USED A HEAD OF A BIRD AND A WOMAN'S LEGS CUT OUT OF MAGAZINES AND STUCK THEM ONTO COLORED PAPER TO MAKE A STRANGE NEW CREATURE.

PHOTO MONTAGE

COMBINE TWO OR MORE PHOTOGRAPHS BY CUTTING
THEM UP AND JOINING THEM TOGETHER IN A
NEW UNREAL SUBJECT.

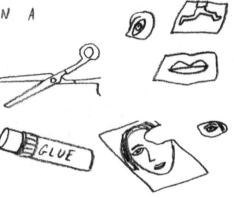

COLLECT OLD NEWSPAPERS AND MAGAZINES. LOOK FOR
INTERESTING FACES, OBJECTS, AND PATTERNS. CUT THEM
OUT AND ARRANGE THEM ON A SHEET OF WHITE OR
COLORED PAPER TO MAKE FACES OR INTERESTING MIXES
OF PEOPLE, CREATURES, AND SHAPES.
WHEN YOU ARE HAPPY WITH THE ARRANGEMENT, STICK
THEM DOWN ONTO A SEPARATE SHEET OF PAPER.

TRY TO MAKE THE
EDGES OF THE SHAPES
FIT TOGETHER. IT WILL
HELP TO MAKE YOUR
PHOTOMONTAGE MORE
CONVINCING.
↓

TRY SOME OF YOUR OWN PHOTOMONTAGES HERE.

NOW DRAW SOME OF YOUR OWN
TO JOIN THE "PARTY."

COMPLETE THESE COLLAGES. YOU CAN USE CUTOUTS FROM NEWSPAPERS AND MAGAZINES, OR YOU CAN DRAW.

Katsushika Hokusai

AFTER
HOKUSAI

HOKUSAI IS BEST KNOWN FOR HIS 200-YEAR-OLD SERIES OF WOODBLOCK
PRINTS CALLED "THIRTY-SIX VIEWS OF MOUNT FUJI," WHICH INCLUDES
THE ICONIC PRINT "THE GREAT WAVE OFF KANAGAWA." IT'S NOT SO
EASY TO MAKE A WOODBLOCK PRINT, AS YOU NEED SPECIAL EQUIPMENT,
BUT THERE ARE MANY WAYS TO MAKE DIFFERENT KINDS OF PRINTS.
I MADE THIS ONE OF MOUNT FUJI USING SIMPLE FOAM PRINTING.

SIMPLE PRINTING

HOKUSAI WAS A MASTER OF WOODBLOCK PRINTING.
YOU CAN MAKE INTERESTING "BLOCK-TYPE" PRINTS BY USING
MATERIALS FOUND AROUND THE HOUSE. HERE ARE SOME
EXAMPLES:

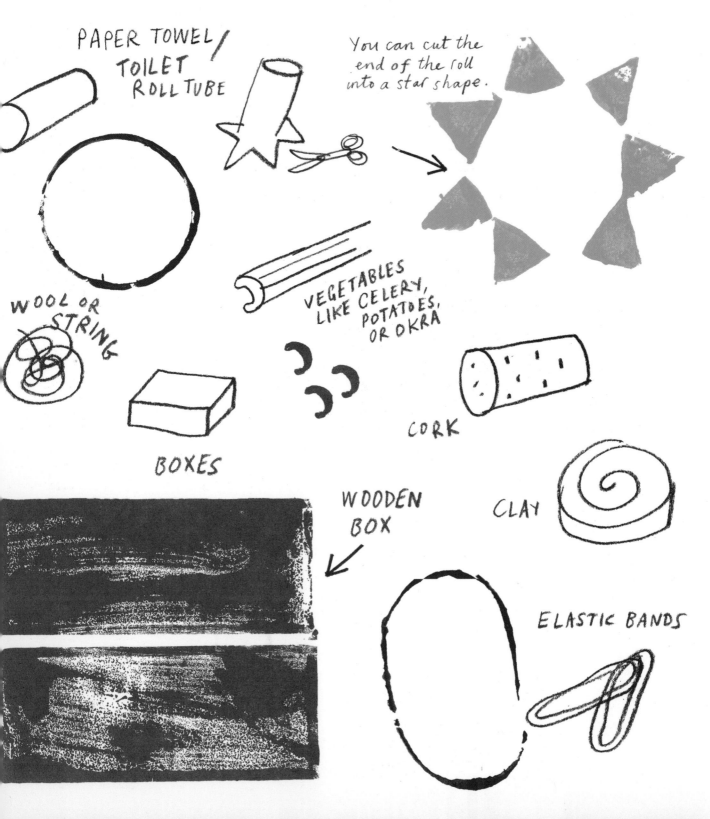

PAPER TOWEL/
TOILET
ROLL TUBE

You can cut the
end of the roll
into a star shape.

WOOL OR
STRING

BOXES

VEGETABLES
LIKE CELERY,
POTATOES,
OR OKRA

CORK

CLAY

WOODEN
BOX

ELASTIC BANDS

BOXES

LIDS

EDGE OF CARDBOARD

STRING PRINTING

1. WRAP THE WOOL OR STRING AROUND A BOX OR LID AND SECURE WITH TAPE

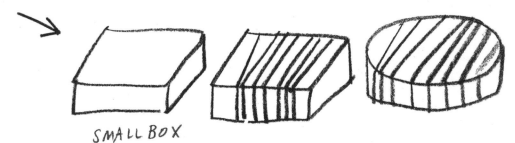

SMALL BOX

2. DIP THE LID OR BOX INTO A SMALL TRAY FILLED WITH POSTER PAINT.

3. NOW PRESS (PRINT) ONTO A SHEET OF WHITE PAPER.

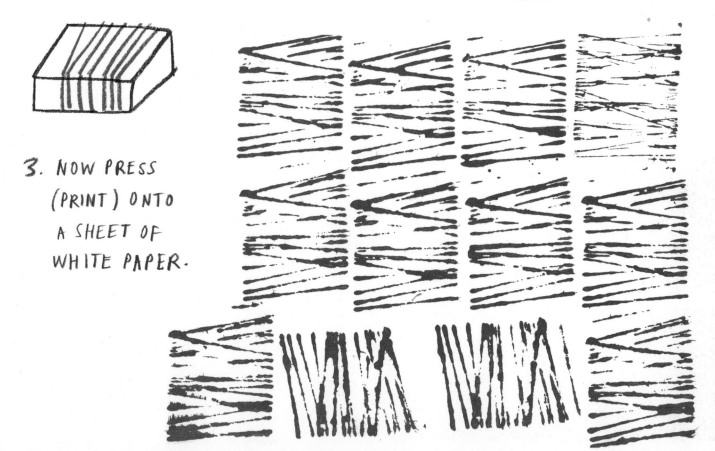

PRACTICE PRINTING

SEE WHAT YOU CAN FIND AROUND YOU.
PAINT OR DIP WITH COLOR AND PRINT HERE.

FOAM PRINTING

CRAFT FOAM IS VERY GOOD FOR PRINTING WITH. YOU CAN ROLLER PAINT ONTO IT AND PRINT LOVELY TEXTURES. YOU CAN ALSO DRAW ON THE FOAM BY PRESSING INTO IT WITH A PENCIL OR SHARP TOOL.

WHAT YOU NEED

SHARP PENCIL OR PEN
CRAFT FOAM
POSTER PAINT
PAPER PALETTE (OR NEWSPAPER)
ROLLER
PAPER
SCRAP PAPER

POST PAIN

FOAM

SCRAP PAPER

FOAM

PRESS HARD, INDENTING THE FOAM

PAPER PALETTE

ROLL OVER FOAM

WHITE PAPER

RUB FIRMLY

1. WITH A SHARP PENCIL OR OLD PEN (WITH NO INK) DRAW YOUR WAVE OR PATTERN IMAGE ONTO THE FOAM. PRESS HARD.
2. NOW ROLLER THE FOAM WITH PAINT.
3. PUT A SHEET OF CLEAN WHITE PAPER ON TOP AND RUB EVENLY WITH THE PALM OF YOUR HAND. PEEL OFF THE PAPER TO REVEAL YOUR BLOCK PRINT.
4. REPEAT AS MANY TIMES AS YOU LIKE.

REMEMBER: YOUR IMAGE, ONCE PRINTED, WILL BE IN REVERSE AND A NEGATIVE IMAGE OF THE ORIGINAL.

YOU CAN ALSO CUT THE FOAM SHAPE OUT AND USE TO PRINT A REPEAT PATTERN.

PRACTICE PRINTING

PRINT YOUR OWN PICTURE HERE USING FOAM OR FOUND OBJECTS.

↘

THE WATER PATTERN OF THIS PRINT WAS MADE WITH A RECTANGULAR FOAM
SHAPE INKED WITH BLUE GOUACHE PAINT, THEN PRESSED, PAINT SIDE DOWN,
ONTO WHITE PAPER.
CAN YOU COMPLETE THE PICTURE? YOU COULD PRINT YOUR OWN MOUNTAIN,
SUN, OR A BOAT ON TOP OF THE WATER.

PRINT YOUR OWN PICTURE HERE USING FOAM OR FOUND OBJECTS.
YOU CAN ADD TO IT BY DRAWING ON TOP ONCE DRY.

Gustav Klimt

GUSTAV KLIMT WAS AN AUSTRIAN PAINTER WHO PAINTED FACES IN A
REALISTIC STYLE BUT WITH THE DRESS AND BACKGROUND FULL OF
PATTERNS MADE FROM RICH COLORS. HE EVEN USED REAL GOLD
LEAF IN HIS PAINTINGS, WHICH MADE THEM SHINE AND SHIMMER. IN
THIS IMAGE OF A SLEEPING PERSON, I'VE BEEN INSPIRED BY KLIMT
TO PAINT A FACE AND HAND IN THE UPPER CORNER, WITH A SWIRLING,
SWEEPING FIELD OF GOLD, BLACK, AND RED PATTERNING THAT IS BOTH
A BLANKET AND AN IMAGE OF THE PERSON'S DREAMING MIND.

COLOR ME IN USING YELLOWS (OR GOLD), ORANGE, RED, AND BLACK.

DRAW OR PAINT PATTERNS TO FILL IN THE DRESS AND COAT.
YOU CAN ALSO DECORATE THE BACKGROUND.

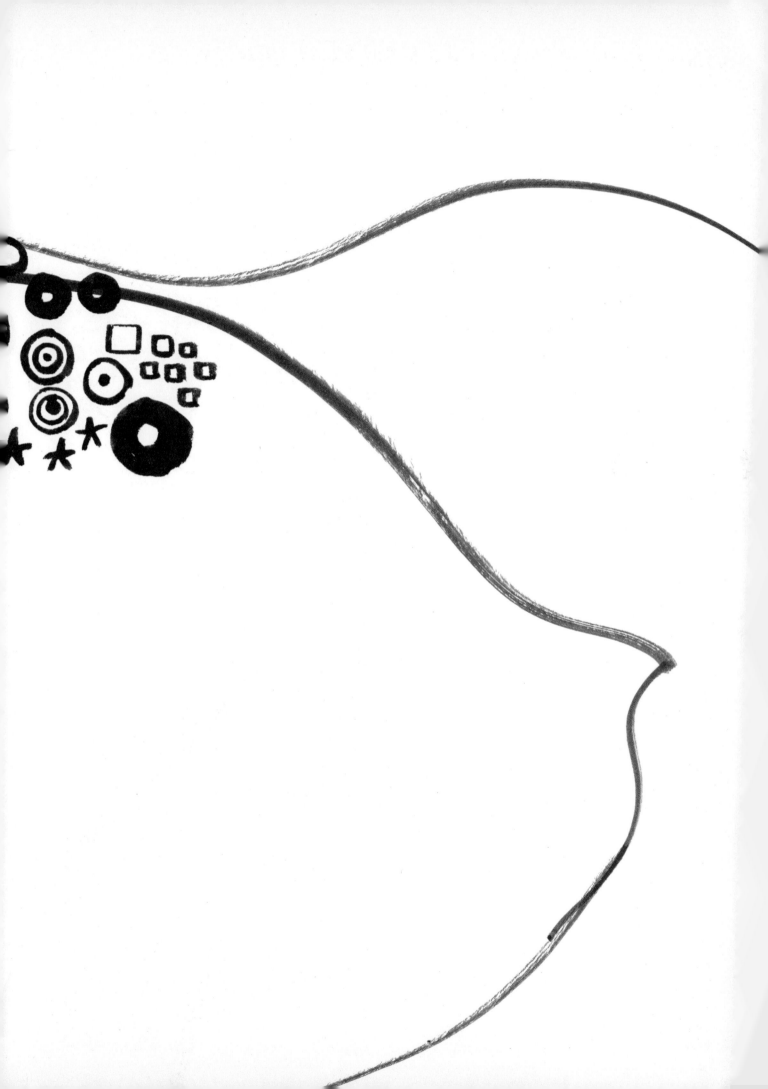

PRINTING GOLD PATTERNS

WHAT YOU NEED

- CRAFT FOAM
- PAPER TRAY OR PALETTE
- GOLD PAINT
- RED and BLACK PAINT
- SCISSORS
- BRUSH OR ROLLER
- WHITE PAPER

CRAFT FOAM

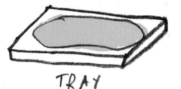

TRAY

1. CUT OUT RECTANGLES AND CIRCLES IN ALL DIFFERENT SIZES.
2. ROLLER PAINT ONTO THE SHAPES AND THEN PRESS DOWN ONTO WHITE PAPER TO "PRINT" THE SHAPE. KEEP THE SHAPES CLOSE TOGETHER.

ONCE SOME OF THE GOLD SHAPES ARE DRY, YOU CAN PRINT RED, BLACK, OR GOLD SHAPES ON TOP.

PRINTED ON TOP

PRINTED ON TOP

NOW DRAW THE HEADS OR FACES
OF YOUR FAMILY IN THE SPACES.
USING FOAM SHAPES, PRINT
PATTERNS AROUND THEM
TO SHOW THEIR CLOTHES
AND BACKGROUND.

TREE OF LIFE

GUSTAV KLIMT PAINTED A "TREE OF LIFE" IN VIBRANT COLORS. THE TREE OF LIFE IS A COMMON SYMBOL IN MANY CULTURES. THE BRANCHES REACHING INTO THE SKY REPRESENT A LINK BETWEEN HEAVEN AND EARTH. THE ROOTS OF THE TREE REPRESENT THE UNDERWORLD.

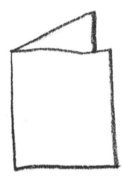

1. FOLD YOUR PAPER IN HALF.

2. DRAW HALF A TREE ON ONE SIDE OF THE PAPER WITH A SOFT PENCIL.

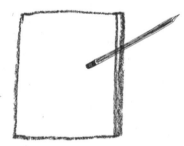

3. FOLD PAPER CLOSED AND RUB HARD WITH THE END OF A PENCIL, GOING OVER ALL THE LINES.

4. THERE WILL BE A FAINT COPY OF YOUR DRAWING ON THE OPPOSITE SIDE OF THE PAPER: A MIRROR-IMAGE.

5. GO OVER THESE FAINT LINES WITH YOUR PENCIL. YOU WILL HAVE MADE A TREE WITH SYMMETRICAL BRANCHES.

NOW COLOR THESE IN AND ADD FRUIT OR BIRDS.

David Hockney

DAVID HOCKNEY SAYS "DRAWING IS AN ENHANCED WAY OF LOOKING."
HE HAS MADE A HUGE VARIETY OF WORK BY LOOKING AT THINGS
AND HOW THEY MOVE OR CHANGE, AND RECORDING THEM IN MANY
DIFFERENT WAYS, FROM PAINTING TO PHOTOGRAPHY AND FILM. HERE
I'VE LOOKED AT WATER AS IT MOVES, AND TRIED TO PAINT ITS
SHAPE-SHIFTING PATTERNS.

LOOKING AT WATER

DAVID HOCKNEY MADE MANY STUDIES OF THE WATER IN
HIS SWIMMING POOL. STUDY THE SHAPES AND PATTERNS
IN WATER BY LOOKING AT THE SEA, A RIVER, WATER IN
YOUR BATH, IN A GLASS, OR IN A PHOTOGRAPH.

REVERSE WATER PATTERN

ON THE PREVIOUS PAGE, I PAINTED WHITE WATER PATTERNS ON COLORED PAPER.
YOU CAN DO THIS.

WHAT YOU NEED

WHITE GOUACHE OR POSTER PAINT (*not watercolor, too wet!)
FAT CHINA WHITE PENCIL
COLORED PAPER (OPPOSITE)
PAINTBRUSH (ROUND)
WATER REFERENCE (OR COPY MY DRAWING ABOVE)

1. MIX UP THE PAINT SO THAT IT'S NICE AND WATERED-DOWN (like light cream).

2. LOOK AT EITHER THE DARK OR LIGHT SHAPES AND PATTERNS
   IN THE WATER AND COPY THEM ONTO THE BLUE PAPER HERE. →

PHOTO COLLAGES

DAVID HOCKNEY MADE PHOTO COLLAGES CALLED "JOINERS"
OF PEOPLE, LANDSCAPES, AND OBJECTS.

HIS FIRST JOINERS WERE MADE WITH POLAROID PRINTS, WHICH WERE SQUARE
SHAPED. LATER HE USED REGULAR PHOTO-LAB RECTANGULAR PRINTS. (BUT YOU CAN
PRINT YOUR OWN.) HOCKNEY'S PHOTO COLLAGES ARE VERY MUCH LIKE CUBIST PAINTINGS.
IN CUBIST ARTWORK THE SUBJECT IS SEEN FROM MANY DIFFERENT ANGLES AT THE SAME TIME.

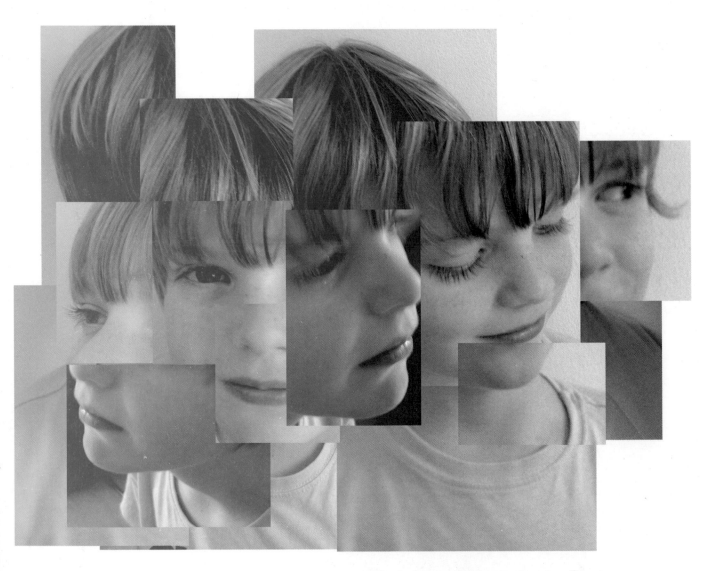

I TOOK 9 PHOTOGRAPHS OF THIS BOY FROM
ALL DIFFERENT ANGLES.
I CUT THEM UP, CROPPING INTO THEM,
THEN I JOINED THEM TOGETHER
LIKE A PUZZLE.

USING A GRID OF SQUARES IS ALSO AN EFFECTIVE WAY OF CREATING A CUBIST, HOCKNEY-LIKE COLLAGE.

I USED SEVERAL PHOTOGRAPHS TO MAKE THIS COLLAGE OF A SWIMMING POOL.

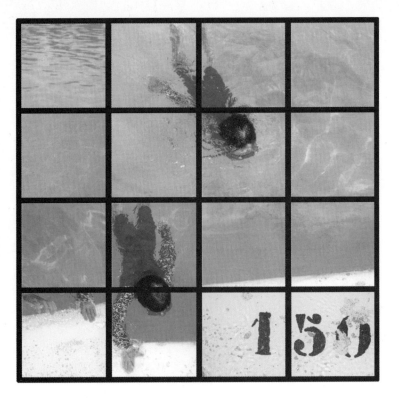

COLLECT PHOTOGRAPHS (OR LOOK FOR PHOTOS FROM MAGAZINES) OF WATER TO COMPLETE THIS
PICTURE. THEY DON'T HAVE TO BE THE SAME BLUE – IN FACT, THE MORE VARIED THE BETTER.
TRY NOT TO LOSE THE BLACK LINE OF THE GRID. THIS HELPS PULL THE IMAGE TOGETHER.

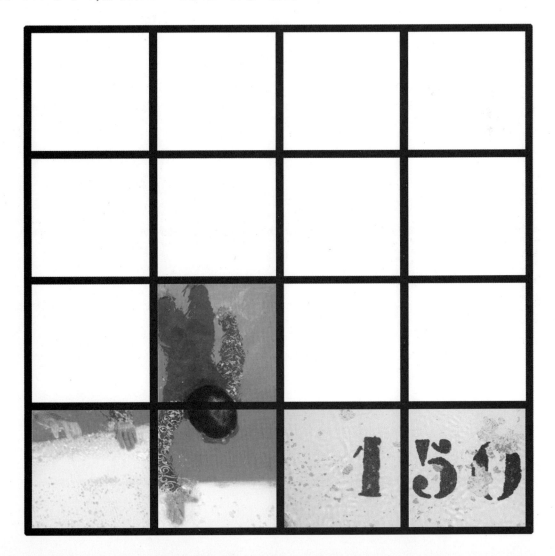

YOU CAN MAKE YOUR OWN PHOTO
COLLAGES. FIND AN INTERESTING
SUBJECT—A PERSON, A LANDSCAPE,
OR A STILL LIFE.

START TAKING PHOTOGRAPHS FROM THE MIDDLE
OF YOUR SUBJECT, MOVING YOUR CAMERA UP AND
DOWN AND TO EITHER SIDE OF YOUR SUBJECT.
TAKE 10-20 PICTURES.
IT'S LIKE YOU'RE MAKING A PUZZLE THAT YOU
WILL JOIN TOGETHER.

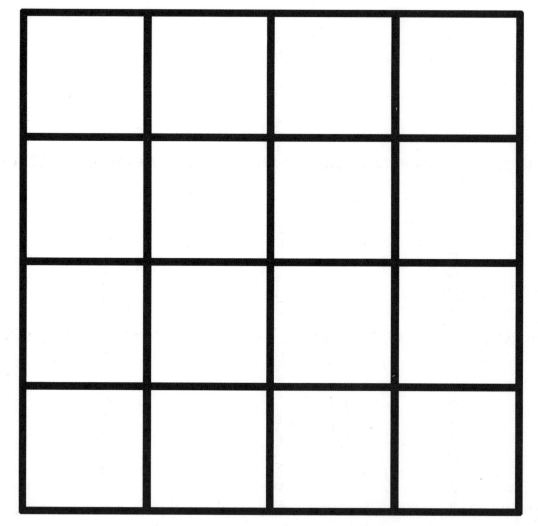

CUT UP YOUR OWN PHOTOS AND FIT THEM ONTO THIS GRID TO CREATE A SENSE OF
MOVEMENT AND PATTERN.

HOCKNEY USES A GRID IN HIS MOST RECENT PAINTINGS. RATHER THAN PAINT ONE HUGE PAINTING, HE PAINTS ON MANY CANVASSES, THEN JOINS THEM ALL TOGETHER (WITHOUT HIDING THE JOINS) TO MAKE HUGE-SCALE PAINTINGS.

CUT UP YOUR OWN DRAWINGS OR PAINTINGS AND FIT THEM ONTO THIS GRID— OR YOU CAN DRAW OR PAINT ON IT. TRY DRAWING A LANDSCAPE OR A PORTRAIT.

COLOR PAPER FOR
CUTTING and STICKING